dissecting MARILYN MANSON

gavin baddeley

dissecting MARILYN MANSON

gavin baddeley

PLEXUS, LONDON

All rights reserved including the right of
reproduction in whole or in part in any form
Copyright © 2000 by Gavin Baddeley
Published by Plexus Publishing Limited
55a Clapham Common Southside
London SW4 9BX
Tel: 020 7622 2440
Fax: 020 7622 2441
First Printing 2000

British Library Cataloguing in Publication Data

Baddeley, Gavin
    Dissecting Marilyn Manson
    1. Marilyn Manson (Musical Group) 2. Rock Musicians - United States - Biography
    I. Title
    782.4' 2'166'0922

    ISBN 0 85965 283 1

Cover photograph by Niels Van Iperen/Retna Ltd
Printed in Great Britain by Hillman Printers
Cover & book design by Phil Gambrill

10 9 8 7 6 5 4 3 2 1

Contents

INTRODUCTION

*T*he pale, scar-crossed, impossibly thin figure of Marilyn Manson looms over the last decade of the twentieth century like some sinister, corset-clad marionette. When, with characteristic bashfulness, he declares that the 1990s have been 'The decade of Marilyn Manson', even his sternest critics have to concede that he's made the transition from rock singer to cultural phenomenon. And critics are not in short supply: from young rock fans who dismiss the flamboyant, self-acclaimed 'Nineties voice of individuality' as a pretentious faggot, to ageing reactionaries of Church and State like Senator Joseph Lieberman, who declared Marilyn Manson, the band, to be 'perhaps the sickest group ever promoted by a mainstream record company'. Governor Frank Keating of Oklahoma was positively apocalyptic when he concluded a rant against the star by dubbing him 'further proof that society's moral values continue to crumble'.

SPLITTING PERSONALITIES

Dissection is the only way to cut through the multiple personalities of a creature that uses them as both camouflage and armour. Nowhere is this better illustrated than in the self-invented identity of Marilyn Manson – with a name split between the theoretical opposites of America's most infamous killer, Charles Manson, and her most beloved Hollywood star, Marilyn Monroe. As their rechristened namesake has observed, 'I thought that those two – positive/negative, male/female, good/evil, beauty/ugliness – created the perfect dichotomy of everything I wanted to represent.'

Of course, the violent disapproval of 'the Establishment' only establishes the band's status in the eyes of their army of fans. As the singer himself observed, 'Deep down most adults hate people who go against the grain. It's comical that people are naïve enough to have forgotten Elvis, Jim Morrison so quickly.' When the authorities try to remove Marilyn Manson from concert bills featuring previously 'unacceptable' acts like Ozzy Osbourne and Nine Inch Nails, it just increases their outlaw credentials. Worse than Ozzy Osbourne, the demonic rocker pursued through the law courts for allegedly recording 'back-masked' messages in the name of Satan! Worse than Trent Reznor's Nine Inch Nails, electronic hatemeisters who recorded their masterpiece on the site of the infamous mass murder of Sharon Tate and her friends!

Such conservative reaction had previously been responsible for introducing the 'parental advisory' stickers – supposedly to dissuade impressionable kids from buying controversial records – that sold so many albums and were worn proudly as T-shirt emblems and tattoos by rebellious youth. Attempts to ban Marilyn Manson gigs are just 300-foot-tall 'parental advisory' stickers in psychedelic neon. Just as the condemnation of specific albums by his Christian teachers helped Brian Warner (the future Marilyn) select his musical entertainment in his early teens, so a new generation of disaffected teenagers were led to forbidden pleasures by the warnings of their elders. 'I've always enjoyed being hated,' observes the singer, 'the people who hate you make it all worthwhile. On my *Antichrist Superstar* tour, I think I upset all the right people; even if people are angry at me, at least they're talking about Marilyn Manson, and I've succeeded.' The truth is that he not only withstands the blizzard of bile directed at him but feeds upon it, growing stronger with each outpouring. Combine this with a mainline into the world's commercial arteries, courtesy of Trent Reznor's Nothing Records, and we have the toxic cocktail that is Marilyn Manson – from obscure Floridan cult band to the cover of *Rolling Stone* in a few short years. But does it add up to anything more than a combination of slick marketing and shock tactics?

Marilyn Manson's critics in the rock media are inclined to dismiss him as just another Iggy Pop, Alice Cooper, KISS, or whatever rock'n'roll animal was rattling the bars of respectability when they were adolescents. Indeed, when asked about originality, Marilyn conceded that 'nothing is really ever new. It's a reinvention of a kind, as everything is these days. Everything comes back eventually, but whatever trend is reinvented it's always with a different angle.' Decadent behaviour and popular music have a far more enduring relationship than most of his critics seem aware. Classical icons like Mozart and Paganini – posthumously elected to the ranks of respectability – led lives of sex, substance abuse and Satanism that make many modern musical monsters seem mild by comparison.

Neither is the idea that shock tactics sell an invention of the contemporary marketplace. Russian composer Igor Stravinsky's savage classical work *Le Sacre du Printemps* (*The Rite of Spring*) was inspired by a vision of a girl dancing herself to death at a pagan rite. (Satanist Blanche Barton includes it among her list of satanic music in her history of the Church of Satan.)

PORTRAIT OF AN AMERICAN FAMILY

Marilyn Manson's 1994 debut album, *Portrait of an American Family*, appeared as the first release for Nothing Records – the label run by Trent Reznor, best known as the harsh but well-respected industrial act Nine Inch Nails. It was initially produced by Roli Mossiman of New York noise legends the Swans, but Marilyn himself dismissed the original mix as too clean and polished. Reznor, working on his angst-classic *Downward Spiral* at the time, agreed to take over the production. The result is industrial rock blended with more gothic playfulness than Reznor would ever allow himself on his own projects. Its pathological exuberance doesn't always hide the technical limitations, but it's good, contagious, toxic fun all the same.

The eponymous lead singer's cheerful doodles of hypodermic syringes and lollipops adorn the sleeve, alongside photos of the band appearing like nascent shadows of the goth-androgynes who later haunted countless magazine covers. The label vetoed Marilyn's plan to include pictures of himself naked as a child, and a faked polaroid of his horribly mutilated girlfriend, on the inside cover – though they reluctantly allowed a curious, nursery rhyme-like piece entitled 'My Monkey', based on a song by Charles Manson, to remain.

'I wanted to address the hypocrisy of talk show America,' explained the band's figurehead, 'how morals are worn as a badge to make you look good and how it's much easier to talk about your beliefs than to live up to them. I was very much wrapped up in the concept that as kids growing up, a lot of the things that we're presented with have deeper meaning than our parents would like us to see, like *Willy Wonka* and the Brothers Grimm.' Conceding it was a bleak album, despite his allusions to children's literature, he added that 'there's a lot of moments of true pessimism, but I think in the end there is a shred of light at the end of the tunnel . . .'

The piece debuted in Paris, 1913, causing a riot. Valentine Gross, a ballet tutor present at the event, observed, 'Nothing that has ever been written about the battle of *Le Sacre du Printemps* has given a faint idea of what actually took place. The theatre seemed to be shaken by an earthquake. It seemed to shudder. People shouted insults, howled and whistled, drowning the music. There was slapping and even punching. Words are inadequate to describe such a scene.' Stravinsky himself gave a more candidly revealing insight: 'After the "performance", we were excited, angry, disgusted and . . . happy.' The head of the ballet company declared the riot to have been 'Exactly what I wanted.'

After a 1999 Marilyn Manson show in Munich degenerated into a riot, when the characteristically-petulant frontman abandoned the stage citing 'technical problems', he later observed: 'I think, if I was a person and I went to a concert, if I had the chance to have a riot, I would be happier to have a riot than to see a concert. That's something they'll remember their whole lives. I'm glad no-one got hurt, but I think a riot's good. Chaos is always important in music.'

According to its main man, there's more to the whole Marilyn Manson sideshow than albums, gigs and cynical money-making. And it's true that there are interesting cultural parallels beneath the surface – such as the striking resemblance between the 'affidavits' issued by the American Family Association, describing blasphemous excesses supposedly occurring at Marilyn Manson gigs, and the descriptions of witches' sabbaths contained in the witch-hunting manuals of medieval Europe. As Manson fan Paula O'Keefe observes in her perceptive article on the Antichrist archetype, 'Apokalypsis', the affidavits are 'Nearly pornographic in their detail and encyclopaedic in their debauchery – drugs, nudity, oral sex, anal sex, bestiality, paedophilia, masturbation, voyeurism, violent rape, bloodshed, full Satanic Mass complete with gory baptism – they quite frankly read like personal fantasies, not only of what a really Satanic rock show would be like but of everything nice people dread yet find fascinating.'

Similar pathological fantasies fuelled witch-hunters' descriptions of the witches' sabbath four centuries before, with the same ingredients of perverse sex, bloodshed, drug abuse and devil-worship. Just as Marilyn Manson concerts are not mythical events, however, containing elements which fundamentalist Christians find genuinely offensive, so some historians are coming to the conclusion that the witches' sabbath *did* take place – even if it was exaggerated by Christian opponents. Perhaps, just as their persecutors claimed, medieval witches were trying to 'turn the whole world upside down' with their deviant sexuality, demonic spirituality and political nihilism.

But even so, surely any connection between Marilyn Manson's performances and the blasphemies of the witch cult are nothing more than coincidence? Perhaps not. An early band newsletter reproduced a Renaissance woodcut of a witches' sabbath. (The US postal service used the illustration to support a legal objection to handling Marilyn Manson merchandise, claiming that a detail of witches boiling children was 'inciting people to cut other people up and boil them'.) The band's debut album also featured the song 'Dogma',

SMELLS LIKE CHILDREN

A curious follow-up to Marilyn Manson's debut success, the 1995 EP *Smells Like Children* is wildly uneven, and was charged by critics as being an ill-conceived cash-in. Marilyn himself described it as 'an EP of remixes, cover songs and audio experiments to encapsulate our mind-set at the time, which was dark, chaotic and drug-addled . . . It was like stitching together an elaborate outfit for a party but catching the hem on a nail and watching helplessly as it unravelled and fell apart.' He claimed its theme of 'use and abuse' made it a disturbing sort of children's record, 'seeing everything from a child's point of view . . . Grand and ugly at times, *Smells Like Children* is almost a metaphor for me trying to hold onto my childhood.'

Almost suicidally self-indulgent, the inane audio experiments and dearth of fresh material were countered, as far as early Spooky Kids were concerned, by abrasive remixes of Marilyn Manson favourites by Dave Ogilvie (from trauma and terror merchants Skinny Puppy) and the Manson catalogue of in-jokes and veiled references. One of the covers, a dark rendition of the Eurythmics' 'Sweet Dreams' which brought the song's disturbing aspects – 'Some of them want to abuse you, some of them want to be abused' – to the fore, introduced the band to the MTV generation and became a surprise success.

Established Spooky Kids were less than impressed by the track's popularity, derisively dubbing new fans 'Sweet Dreamers', whereas Marilyn had always wanted to infect the mainstream with his personal brand of decadence, deeming this more accessible offering 'a clever piece of cheese on a rat trap'. With typical perversity, Marilyn Manson's weakest release was the one that launched the band on the yellow brick road to superstardom.

with the refrain 'burn the witches', which Marilyn later explained was 'from their point of view. The phrase "burn the witches" is spoken in a sarcastic tone . . . the song is about persecution.'

The lead singer's lyrics and graphics invite speculation about their meaning – he obviously loves word games, puzzles, obscure connections and in-jokes. The Internet is full of sites established by Spooky Kids (borrowed from the original band name – Marilyn Manson and the Spooky Kids), as dedicated fans style themselves, devoted to deciphering his oblique references and diverse allusions. Part of the motivation for this book is to explore these references, and put them into their cultural context.

Dissecting Marilyn Manson is not centrally about the band's music – while I'm not ignoring it, it's seldom the most interesting part of the Marilyn Manson package. As Marilyn himself observed in a 1998 interview, 'Once I assumed the role as a villain, the whole thing stopped being about music. I had started out just exploring something, and pretty soon it was having this effect in politics and culture. It raised conversations in families and churches.'

The man behind the bizarre composite name is not a musician, but a rock star who rarely refers to his work in standard musical terms, preferring to describe his creative output as performance art or, more interestingly, 'science projects'. Images are conjured forth of a mischievous schoolboy with a chemistry set, or Dr Frankenstein calling down lightning from the heavens to bring his blasphemous creation to life, and both are equally true. Marilyn Manson is a monster stitched together from the pieces of a thousand other creatures. This book will pick open some of that stitching.

Before he was a rock star, Brian Warner was a rock writer who tried to find his voice reading poetry at an open mike spot in a small club in Miami. However, the most potent vehicle for making a statement in modern America is not poetry, or journalism, but rock'n'roll and music journalism only convinced him that his destiny lay in being the subject – rather than the author – of rock interviews: 'Nobody had anything to say. I felt that I should be answering the questions instead of asking them. I wanted to be the other side of the pen.'

Many writers-turned-performers (most rock newspapers are staffed by frustrated musicians) tend to be more considered in their approach than their rivals. Marilyn Manson is, in this sense, a vehicle for the ideas and obsessions of the artist formerly known as Brian Warner. 'I approach it as an art form,' he has explained. 'A lot of people perceived it as a product and that's why rock'n'roll has been so safe and boring, I want to take it and make it into a religion, make it into an art.'

The eponymous Marilyn regards publicity and interviews not as a distraction from his work, but as a vital part of it. His ready wit and talent for lurid melodramatics ensure that many editors and broadcasters – while contemptuous of his shameless showmanship, and wilful advocacy of the unfashionable – can't resist giving coverage to this perverse harlequin.

ANTICHRIST SUPERSTAR

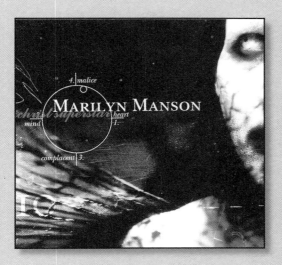

Recorded during a traumatic period in Marilyn Manson's life, the 1996 album *Antichrist Superstar* was his most assured and ambitious project to date, though largely devoid of the poisonous playfulness of earlier recordings. As a densely-layered industrial concept album in three cycles, it follows the metamorphosis of the vulnerable human Wormboy into the merciless superhuman Antichrist Superstar.

Marilyn applied his passion for puzzles and coincidences to the occultic disciplines of numerology and the Kabbala 'to create a musical ritual that will bring about the Apocalypse'. With ritualised degeneracy and deviant philosophy, he blurred the barriers between art and reality to birth a truly bizarre creation. Something like a Hammer horror remake of Pink Floyd's *The Wall*, or David Bowie's *Ziggy Stardust* album produced by Aleister Crowley, '*Antichrist Superstar* was a study about the abuse of power,' testified its creator, 'about rock 'n roll, religion and politics.'

Trent Reznor produced once again, though by now their relationship was becoming strained. 'I saw *Antichrist Superstar* as essentially a pop album,' explained the band's main man, 'albeit an intelligent, complex and dark one. I wanted to make something as classic as the records I had grown up on. Trent seemed to have his heart set on breaking new ground as a producer and recording something experimental, an ambition that often ran in direct opposition to the tunefulness, coherence and scope I insisted on . . . *Antichrist Superstar* was about using your power, not your misery, and watching that power destroy you and everyone around you.' The themes called for dark, bombastic showmanship, in contrast to the savage introspection that characterised Nine Inch Nails. Marilyn Manson stuck to his guns, and was rewarded with a hugely successful album that established the aspirent Antichrist as a superstar.

MECHANICAL ANIMALS

Released in 1998, *Mechanical Animals* caught both fans and critics by surprise. With Trent Reznor absent from the production booth for the first time, the industrial edge and gothic kitsch of previous releases were replaced by an urbane glam rock feel, topped with a charge of synthesised cynicism – an album 'with more skin and nerves'. Marilyn's new twin personae for this musical exploration of the hollowness of fame, was that of an impossibly decadent rock star and an androgynous extraterrestrial. Musically, the album pays shameless tribute to theatrical and glam rock gods of the past, from David Bowie to Gary Numan, via Marc Bolan and Pink Floyd.

Perversely, the same critics who lambasted previous Marilyn Manson releases for being derivative lauded *Mechanical Animals*, which wore its influences prominently on its sleeve. Some fans mourned the loss of the overt darkness of the MM *oeuvre*, and, while it sold well, *Mechanical Animals* was not the phenomenon that *Antichrist Superstar* had been. No doubt anticipating such a response, its creator was always careful to explain that *Mechanical Animals* was a sequel to *Antichrist Superstar*, part of a progression.

'Whatever I do musically is always kind of a reflection of my personal life,' he explained. '*Antichrist Superstar* was a very cold, numb transformation and the result was a rebirth in some ways. *Mechanical Animals* documents the feeling coming back. It's like a leg that was asleep and now it's starting to tingle. This record is like me coming to terms with the pain and fear of being human for the first time. It's not a regretful record, but it's kind of [about] living in a world that you don't belong in for the first time.'

Almost apologetically, Marilyn countered the idea that his synth-pop album was an altogether brighter, lighter experience: 'To me, it is a pretty depressing record, and at times when it leads you to believe it's not depressing, it's being intentionally fake and sarcastic. The elements of glam are very ironic. I think the more people begin to listen to it, they'll see that – the dark. When things are expressed innocuously – that's when they're most depressing.'

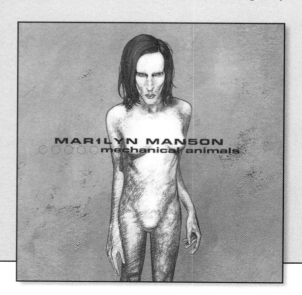

When speaking with some of the legions of teenagers in Marilyn Manson T-shirts, wanting to know just what fascinated these Spooky Kids about their idol, I was surprised at how many of them mentioned figures like Friedrich Nietzsche – the nineteenth-century German philosopher best known for his 'God is dead!' dictum, one of a number of figures who presided over what one writer recently described as *God's Funeral*. Even Marilyn Manson's most cynical detractors admit that there's something intriguing about a performer who can drum up interest amongst a generation of disaffected adolescents in the philosophers who undermined Christian belief, paving the way for twentieth-century atheism and the Satanism that will mark this new millennium. A minister of the Church of Satan, Manson regularly alludes to these iconoclastic thinkers, whose relevance will be examined in greater detail.

As important as the philosophical assault upon Christianity was the 'Decadent' movement that emerged from within the artistic community in Paris during the late nineteenth century – a loose grouping of artists, poets and novelists with a powerful conviction that everything was going to hell, and an equally powerful determination to enjoy the ride. Dedicated to extremes of experience and sensation – both beautiful and horrific – they held a casual disregard for common sense, morality and even sanity.

In his book *Decadence and Catholicism*, American academic Ellis Hanson says that 'the decadents cultivated a fascination with all that was commonly perceived as unnatural or degenerate, with sexual perversity, nervous illness, crime, and disease, all presented in a highly aestheticized context calculated to subvert or, at any rate, to shock conventional morality. Both stylistically and thematically, decadence is an aesthetic in which failure and decay are regarded as seductive, mystical, or beautiful . . . The typical decadent hero is, with a few exceptions, an upper-class, overly educated, impeccably dressed aesthete, a man whose masculinity is confounded by his tendency to androgyny, homosexuality, masochism, mysticism, or neurosis.'

Marilyn Manson may qualify as one of the 'few exceptions' in not being a member of the upper classes (though he is an American media star, which makes him a part of the new aristocracy) and being self-educated rather than 'overly educated'. Aside from that however, this description fits him like a rubber dress. As he acknowledged in a Dutch interview to promote the *Mechanical Animals* album, 'Decadence is a very strong side of my personality . . . It's also a way to make things clear. By exaggerating, by magnifying subjects you can pass on your intention in the right way. Apart from that I am just somebody who's up for everything, to experiment with things and to discover things, even if it was just only to test your own inner powers.'

Speaking of his admiration for the famous Anglo-Irish decadent Oscar Wilde, Marilyn quoted the seminal decadent doctrine of 'The idea of art for the sake of art.' He might just as appropriately have come out with Wilde's observation that 'My existence is scandal.' The crowning scandal of Wilde's life was his 1895 conviction and subsequent imprisonment for homosexuality, at a time when it was still a criminal offence. Recalling

THE LONG HARD ROAD OUT OF HELL

the long hard road out of hell
MARILYN MANSON
WITH NEIL STRAUSS

The 1998 autobiography *The Long Hard Road Out of Hell* belongs among the Marilyn Manson canon just as much as the band's recordings. Written in conjunction with *Rolling Stone* journalist Neil Strauss (who got to share a little MM-excess and scandal as a result), it covers the metamorphosis of plain old Brian Warner, from his childhood in suburban Ohio, to his rebirth as the Antichrist Superstar, and the accompanying, controversy-strewn Dead to the World tour in 1996. In this sense, it's a companion volume to *Antichrist Superstar*, sharing the album's division into three parts with its distinctive, artfully-grotesque visual style.

The book also lays bare some of the in-jokes and esoterica of *Antichrist Superstar*, previously only understood by a few of the faithful. Black magician Aleister Crowley – a profound influence on Marilyn Manson – always put great store by his apprentices keeping detailed magical diaries, and parts of the autobiography read like just such a record of excess. Repellent yet compelling, *The Long Hard Road Out of Hell* is a powerful piece of decadent art in its own right. While by no means universally admired, it sold in vast numbers (underlining the unusual literacy of Spooky Kids, compared to the average rock fan), whilst, at the same time, confirming to his critics that Marilyn was an articulate force to be reckoned with.

the traumatic episode, Wilde wrote, 'I remember as I was sitting in the dock on the occasion of my last trial . . . being sickened with horror at what I heard. Suddenly it occurred to me, "How splendid it would be, if I was saying all this about myself!"'

One of the most perverse features of Marilyn's career is his determination to evoke disapproval, even disgust, to a degree that goes beyond his ambition to be 'America's villain'. Nowhere is this more in evidence than in his autobiography, *The Long Hard Road Out of Hell*, which is not so much a candid confession as a self-inflicted character assassination – he even includes the worst libels aimed at him by his enemies as a kind of perverse appendix. As vicious as he is towards many of the figures he describes, few come out of it looking worse than the author himself, at the centre of one sordid incident after another.

Once again, we find echoes of this behaviour in the lives of the Decadents. Ellis Hanson considered the case of the poet Baudelaire, who lived scandalously but wanted people to think his life more scandalous still, quoting one of his letters: '"Being chaste as paper, sober as water, devout as a woman at communion, harmless as a sacrificial lamb, it would not displease me to be taken for a debauchee, a drunkard, an infidel and a murderer." The likelihood that he was none of the former and some of the latter is immaterial. He eagerly invited upon himself the sensations of shame, guilt, remorse, hatred, and ennui in a self-conscious cultivation of abjection that had little if anything to do with actual crimes. Although his life was scandalous, he still exaggerated his crimes in an effort at provocation.'

Or, as Marilyn Manson says: 'The thing with rumours is that it doesn't matter whether or not they are true, because it is what's popular that everybody believes. No matter how many times you can say no, everybody still thinks something different. I've never minded the rumours, at least the people are talking. I think if people weren't talking, then I would have something to worry about. A lot of the times the reality of Marilyn Manson wasn't enough for the conservative Christian angle to really suppress what I do.'

Marilyn enjoys his villainy, encouraging dark rumours that his enemies will repeat and amplify. Ironically, they become the best PR agents he could hope for, leaving him looking like the persecuted scapegoat and themselves like hysterical liars. And they fall for it time and time again.

Chapter One
MEET THE FAMILY

*T*he future Marilyn Manson was born in 1969 and christened Brian Warner. It was to be a pivotal year in American history, the year hippie culture reached its zenith at the Woodstock festival in New York State.

Harvard psychology professor-turned LSD guru Timothy Leary later wrote, in his essay on 'The Woodstock Generation', that 'the "Woodstock experience" became the role model for the counterculture of that time. The Summer of Love kids went on to permanently change American culture with principles that the Soviets in 1989 called glasnost and perestroika. Hippies started the ecology movement. They combated racism. They liberated sexual stereotypes, encouraged change, individual pride and self-confidence.' He went on to compare Woodstock to the rites of the Ancient Greek god of wine, Dionysus, describing the festival as 'the greatest pagan, Dionysian rock'n'roll musical event ever performed, with plenty of joyous nudity, and wall-to-wall psychedelic sacraments. And click on this: not one act of recorded violence!'

Twenty-five years on, the Woodstock festival was revived – but with little for the 'Summer of Love' children to groove to. Young rock fans had replaced the peace sign with the devil's horns signal, and most agreed the show had been stolen by a band named Nine Inch Nails promoting the album *Pretty Hate Machine*. The original festival had resulted in upstate New York being declared an official disaster area – the naïveté or incompetence of the hippies resulting in disastrously inadequate facilities. The thirtieth anniversary festival, in 1999, had to be stormed by riot police. Timothy Leary had overlooked the fact that the wild revels of Dionysus he evoked involved not only sex and intoxication, but also violence: twelve tractor-trailers were destroyed, speaker towers toppled and concession stands looted, as festival-goers danced through fires that rapidly burnt out of control. And click on this: more than half-a-dozen rapes reported!

Marilyn Manson had been scheduled to play the 1999 Woodstock Festival, but declined when a suitable time-slot could not be found. As the British music paper *NME* observed: 'Fact: while the original Woodstock Festival – high-watermark of the sixties idealism of peace, love and good music – was taking place in 1969, Marilyn's namesake

WINDOWS ON THE SOUL

Perhaps the most striking illustration of the marriage of opposites in Marilyn Manson are his mismatched eyes. This is a pervasive theme: in *The Long Hard Road Out of Hell* he says that both his childhood pet, a dog named Aleusha, and the cat belonging to his girlfriend Missi had naturally mismatched eyes; David Bowie, an important early inspiration, has one discoloured eye due to a fight at school; in the 1976 Antichrist horror-fantasy *The Omen* (which scared little Brian Warner as a child), when Evil drives the Holy Spirit from a possessed priest it is said to escape through one of his eyes, changing its colour.

Many of those who attributed hypnotic, or even magical, powers to Charles Manson also believed they were contained within his penetrating stare. On a contemporary level, coloured contact lenses are a fashionable form of body-modification – albeit a subtler, less visceral version than the tattooing or piercing normally associated with the modern primitive cult.

Charles was preparing for his dune buggy attack battalions to put an end to the hippy dream in a blood soaked orgy of slaughter in the Hollywood Hills. Perhaps the irony was not lost on the organisers of Woodstock '99.'

When articulating the concept behind Marilyn Manson on MTV, its frontman explained, 'I was writing a lot of lyrics five or six years ago, and the name Marilyn Manson I thought really describes everything that I had to say. You know, male and female, beauty and ugliness, and it was just very American. It was a statement on the American culture, the power that we give to icons like Marilyn Monroe and Charles Manson and since that's where it's always gone from there. It's about the paradox. Diametrically opposed archetypes.'

All of Marilyn Manson's early members followed the same formula for choosing stage names, adopting the christian name of a female sex symbol or starlet and the surname of a notorious male murderer. Marilyn Manson, however, was always destined to be the most memorable, marrying two icons at opposite extremes of twentieth century culture. Marilyn Monroe is a screen legend whose immense popularity and potent sexual magnetism, frozen in time forever by her untimely death in 1962, have turned her into the most powerful contemporary goddess of love and lust. Public revulsion at the crimes of Charles Manson, convicted of ordering his hippie 'Family' to conduct a series of atrocities in 1969, have made him into an icon of incomparable intensity, a devil figure symbolising hatred and death.

'I watch a lot of talk shows,' the 1990s Marilyn later observed, 'and I was struck by how they lumped together Hollywood starlets with serial killers, just bringing everything to the same sensational level. But Monroe had a dark side with her drugs and depression, and Manson had a true message and charisma for his followers, so it's not all black and white.'

Manson felt compelled to clarify his position when defending himself against

SEX KITTENS WITH CLAWS

In his autobiography, musing on the origins of his moniker, Marilyn Manson laments that 'people always ask me about the darker half of my name but never about Marilyn Monroe'. To be fair, neither Monroe's singing, nor the dialogue from her films, ever surface regularly in Marilyn Manson material the way that quotes from Charlie Manson do. Her importance is as an icon, a symbol of beauty and lust, though – as the contemporary Marilyn is quick to point out – this Hollywood legend also has a darker aspect. This is evident in her largely light-hearted acting career: *The Asphalt Jungle* (1950) and *Niagara* (1955) belong in the gritty *noir* genre, while her popular comedy *Some Like it Hot* (1958) is a cross-dressing farce played out against the grim background of the St. Valentine's Day massacre.

Marilyn Monroe – Hollywood's tragic love goddess – with friend.

As a girl who achieved the American dream of rags-to-riches, but lived a largely miserable life, there's something faintly unsavoury about Monroe's onscreen persona. She was a sex symbol who – unlike more upfront or sophisticated Hollywood vamps – cloaked her sexuality in a feigned childishness which, at times, suggested an almost paedophilic appeal. Before her Hollywood break she worked on the fringes of the pornography trade, famously posing nude for a calendar. Later, after becoming successful, she became addicted to drugs.

Anton LaVey, Marilyn Manson's spiritual godfather, claimed to have had an affair with the pre-stardom Monroe, at the very beginning of the 1950s. In his biography, *The Secret Life of a Satanist*, author Blanche Barton observes that, 'In 1973 LaVey wrote in a *Cloven Hoof* article that Marilyn Monroe will become the satanic "Madonna" of the 21st century. In a sense that's already happened. Since her death, she has been fashioned into a goddess . . . Marilyn Monroe is not a goddess pure and sexless, but satanically just the opposite – a fleshy goddess: passionate, flawed, enticing, beautiful.'

As with Marilyn Manson himself, other band members' names have been a hybrid of female sex symbol and all-American mass murderer. Bassist Twiggy Ramirez took the first half of his name from a famous London fashion model of the Swinging Sixties, a short-haired, flat-chested waif who took androgyny into the mainstream. Guitarist Daisy Berkowitz paid tribute to Daisy Duke from Seventies TV series *The Dukes of Hazzard* – in this cheesily subversive show, where the heroes were white trash (normally portrayed as villains or comic relief) who regularly fooled the corrupt local cops and Daisy an adolescent male fantasy in provocatively-brief denim shorts. Original keyboardist Zsa Zsa Speck opted for Zsa Zsa Gabor as a role model – a former Miss Hungary and actress in such uncelebrated crap as *Queen of Outer Space* and *Frankenstein's Great Aunt Tillie*. The epitome of the celebrity who is famous simply for being famous, Zsa Zsa is still considered part of Hollywood's tacky aristocracy.

Current keyboardist Madonna Wayne Gacy adopted the first part of his moniker from the pop star – Ms. Ciccone – rather than the Holy Mother of God. Madonna, like Marilyn Manson, has encountered much criticism from Christian lobbyists, and was denounced as blasphemous by the Vatican for her smoulderingly-erotic 'Like a Prayer' video. When relations between Marilyn Manson and Trent Reznor's Nothing Records became shaky, there was even talk of Madonna signing the band to her Maverick label. This fell apart, however, when the peroxide-blonde pop siren allegedly insisted Madonna Wayne Gacy stop using 'her' name – the delicious irony being the suggestion that the provocative Italian-American singer, apparently indifferent to the offence her stage name gave Roman Catholics, was herself offended by this personal 'blasphemy' against her.

Other starlet namesakes are, perhaps, less obvious. Drummer Ginger Fish owes his first name to Ginger Rogers, the perky Hollywood actress whose overblown song and dance epics partnering Fred Astaire during the 1930s made her a household name. Bassist Gidget Gein took his name from Gidget, the air-headed heroine of a series of unspeakably feeble teen-beach-party movies of the late 1950s and early 1960s. The original Gidget was played by Sandra Dee, described by one critic as 'one of the least interesting teen idols in cinema history', whose only mark on cultural history is a song in the 1978 nostalgic hit Hollywood musical *Grease* ('Look At Me, I'm Sandra Dee').

KING OF THE CREEPY CRAWLERS

On 9 August 1969, police found the bodies of beautiful, heavily-pregnant film star Sharon Tate and four of her friends at her exclusive Beverly Hills mansion. They had been brutally stabbed, bludgeoned and shot, their blood used to daub the walls with the legends 'WAR' and 'PIG'. The following night, a Los Angeles couple named Leno and Rosemary LaBianca were stabbed to death at their suburban home. This time the dripping crimson graffiti read 'DEATH TO PIGS', 'RISE' and 'HEALTER SKELTER' (sic), while 'WAR' had been carved into Leno's stomach. When the perpetrators were caught, to the horror of both 'straight' society and the counterculture, they turned out to be members of a hippie commune calling itself 'the Family'.

Eight members of the Family were found guilty of connected charges, with four sentenced to death (later commuted to life imprisonment) in a controversial courtroom drama that at times resembled a medieval witch trial. Among those receiving the ultimate penalty was a short, bearded ex-con named Charles Manson, who, while not present at the murders, was still found guilty of conspiring in the crimes by virtue of being the Family's nominal leader. To this day his supporters maintain Charlie never killed anyone, while less sympathetic commentators have linked him to as many as 35 unsolved murders. The truth, not least concerning what motivated the horrific Tate-LaBianca massacres, is now swathed in a thick cloak of mind games, drug abuse and modern myth which is devilishly difficult, perhaps impossible, to penetrate.

Charlie Manson was born the illegitimate son of a promiscuous wild child named Kathleen Maddox in 1934. By age twelve, the state had put him into the 'care' of a brutal Catholic boys' home, from whence he graduated, via a life of petty crime, to a series of reform schools and gaols. Despite the appalling abusiveness of these institutions, by the time of his parole in 1967 the jailhouse was Charlie's entire world ('My mother', as he would later claim) and he begged not to be released.

The world Charles Manson found outside was in the grip of the psychedelic revolution. When he drifted to its epicentre on the USA's West Coast, the hippies' free love and drugs blew his mind. But Charlie's mind games, and the survival skills developed in gaol, proved just as mind-blowing to the semi-nomadic 'Family' that assembled around him – not least the young girls who became the unlikely guru's harem. Cleverly, perhaps brilliantly, manipulative, Charlie was also indelibly scarred by his dysfunctional upbringing. Somehow, in August 1969, the cocktail of drugs, frustration and youth rebellion combined with the ex-con's mind-control complex to send the Family spinning into the helter-skelter vortex of violence that shocked the world.

accusations that his own work had inspired an act of mass murder in 1999: 'The name Marilyn Manson has never celebrated the sad fact that America puts killers on the cover of *Time* magazine,' he wrote, 'giving them as much notoriety as our favourite media stars. From Jesse James to Charles Manson, the media, since their inception, have turned criminals into folk heroes.' But whither the thin line between ironic comment and celebration?

The first song on Marilyn Manson's debut album has the opening line 'I am the god of fuck' – a direct quote from Charlie Manson, later appropriated as a title by his new androgynous namesake. Just as some early concerts were peppered with readings from Dr Seuss, others featured quotes from Charles Manson; early promotional material was also littered with references and graphics easily identified with Charlie by the counter-cultural cognoscenti. Marilyn fought hard to keep the song 'My Monkey' – based on the Charles Manson song 'Mechanical Man' – on *Portrait of An American Family*, despite the deep reservations of his record label.

Brian Warner discovered Charlie's music back in high school, buying the killer's notorious *Lie* album. Later, he would integrate Charlie's lyrics into the poems that finally evolved into Marilyn Manson songs. He recalls first becoming intrigued by the notorious criminal via the song 'Mechanical Man', describing its creator as 'a gifted philosopher, more powerful intellectually than those who condemned him. But at the same time, his intelligence (perhaps even more so than the actions he had others carry out for him) made him seem eccentric and crazy, because extremes – whether good or bad – don't fit into society's definition of normality. Though "Mechanical Man" was a nursery rhyme on the surface, it also worked as a metaphor for Aids, the latest manifestation of man's age-old habit of destroying himself with his own ignorance, be it of science, sex or drugs.'

'A gifted philosopher'? Isn't Marilyn Manson – just like the mainstream media he seems to despise – recreating his criminal namesake as a folk hero? Is the criticism of the Reverend Charles 'Tex' Watson – formerly of the Manson Family, now a born-again Christian – that Marilyn Manson is bringing 'the Manson madness into the hearts and minds of millions', valid? If it is, then he is only one of a long tradition of counter-cultural figures who have fallen under the spell of Charles Manson.

At the same time Woodstock '99 was descending into chaos, fashionable photographer Geoffrey Cordner was preparing an exhibition entitled *These Children That Come At You With Knives* for a Hollywood gallery, consisting of a series of staged photos re-enacting the Manson massacres. The roll call of models included members of such hip bands as the MC5, Porno for Pyros, Tool and the New York Dolls. Guns 'n' Roses recorded one of Charlie's compositions, 'Look At Your Game, Girl', on their album *The Spaghetti Incident?* – much to Marilyn Manson's displeasure, as he claimed Axl Rose had stolen his idea of recording a Charles Manson song. (It wasn't only Manson's wrath that the band incurred – Manson victim Sharon Tate's sister Patty was outraged, leading Guns

Discussing Charlie Manson's influence on Marilyn Manson, his namesake explained, 'I think Charles Manson is the greatest rock star of all time. He was all about music. He never even had to have a hit and he's one of the biggest stars that you could ever find. That's something that we can thank America for, whether you like it or not, America put him there.'

Whatever roles Charlie Manson, the mirror man, adopted for those around him, as far as he himself was concerned all he wanted was to be a successful musician. Taught to play guitar in gaol by gangster Alvin 'Creepy' Karpis (former member of the Ma Barker gang and one-time Public Enemy Number One), on his release Charlie used his influence on the hippie scene to try to launch a musical career – even cutting a demo album with members of the Family. (One theory concerning the Tate killings was that the intended target was a record producer, Doris Day's son Terry Melcher, who Charlie believed had discarded him).

Charlie cultivated a friendship with Dennis Wilson, the reckless drummer of sunny surf sensations the Beach Boys. For a while, Manson's Family even lived in Wilson's luxury log cabin on Pacific Palisades, while the Beach Boys recorded one of Charlie's compositions – 'Cease To Exist', suitably sanitised for public consumption as 'Never Learn Not To Love'. But relations with the Family soured, and Charlie's crew was evicted. Charlie responded by sending Wilson a silver bullet, the threat inspiring the Beach Boy to sleep with a gun under his pillow. Meanwhile, Charlie was becoming increasingly fascinated by the Beatles' *White Album*, reading secret messages and odd prophecies into its lyrics. According to some commentators, it was these 'messages' which inspired him to order the 1969 massacres.

The notoriety those crimes attracted finally inspired the underground release of Charlie's demo album, under the title *Lie* (its sleeve a mock-up of the *Life* magazine cover story on the Manson crimes). Over the years, this would be followed by a sporadic series of bootleg releases smuggled out of gaol for a growing cult audience. Charlie's music has been memorably described by Jim Goad as 'an incredibly depressing sonic mix of Hank Williams and the Velvet Underground' – despite this, it continues to attract acclaim from the dark extremes of the musical avant-garde, such as satanic folk-rocker Wendy Van Dusen, of Neither\Neither World, who cites him as a primary influence. Body-building punk poet Henry Rollins spoke about trying to officially release an album of Manson's music during the Eighties, observing, 'He's this five feet four inch guy, sitting behind bars, and he terrifies people.'

'n' Roses to give up any profits from the recording.) There is talk of an animated feature based on Charlie's life and crimes, featuring the voices of bands like White Zombie, L7, the Ramones and Rancid, while – in perhaps the ultimate white-trash tribute – Charlie Manson has already starred in an episode of cartoon show *South Park*.

While Axl and company could plead that they were looking at the Manson myth from an ironic perspective, others on the dark fringes of the counterculture had been more than happy to get their hands bloody. When news originally broke of the arrest of a Californian commune for the horrific Tate-LaBianca murders in 1969, many hippies assumed it was a frame-up orchestrated by the notoriously corrupt LA police. When it became apparent, however, that these unlikely butchers were almost certainly guilty, much of that support melted away, as the Love Generation began to wonder what had happened to their dream. In the words of writer David Dalton (a hippie who initially believed the Manson Family to be innocent), Charlie had killed 'part of ourselves, our Edenic others who had once believed we could create a new heaven and a new earth'. However, a hard core of radicals in the hippie movement continued to hail him as a martyr to their cause, lauding his atrocities as revolutionary acts. Hippie terrorists the Weathermen declared 1969 'The Year of the Fork' in Charlie's honour (one of the victims died with a fork stuck in his belly), and told fellow revolutionaries to 'dig it'.

Charles Manson - the hypnotic hate messiah who heralded the end of the Summer of Love.

Perhaps the most controversial celebration of the Manson murders came from the opposite end of the political spectrum to the long-haired leftists of the Sixties. The 8/8/88 Rally was held in a San Francisco theatre on 8 August 1988 (the anniversary of the Tate slayings), featuring a rare exploitation film based on the Tate massacre entitled *The Other Side of Madness*, sinister avant-garde music and apocalyptic right-wing speeches. Among those leading the proceedings were occult fascist and respected experimental musician Boyd Rice and Zeena LaVey, youngest daughter of the notorious Anton LaVey. Both were prominent members of her father's Church of Satan, an organisation Marilyn Manson was later initiated into with the clerical rank of Reverend.

The reasons given for 'celebrating' the murders are instructive. Firstly, the organisers felt that the Family's 1969 murder spree had killed off the Sixties, ending the Summer of Love in a bloodbath. Nikolas Schreck (a fellow right-wing occultist and partner of Zeena LaVey) explained, 'The Sharon Tate murder was a symbolic representation of the end of an entire way of thought, of compassion for the weak, peace for its own sake, pacifism that breeds stagnation. That entire way of thinking was destroyed on August 8th 1969 and that is why we chose this evening to perform a ritual of cleansing and of purification.'

Considering the hippie movement portrayed itself as a movement of peace and understanding, there has been a surprisingly long line of suspects keen to hold up their hands to the murder of the Love Generation. Iggy Pop, asked what contribution he and his wild proto-punk band the Stooges had made to the Sixties, replied that they 'wiped them out'. Alice Cooper, regarded by some as Marilyn Manson's prototype, is fond of boasting he 'single-handedly drove the stake through the heart of the love generation!' Johnny Rotten, noxious vocalist with punk legends the Sex Pistols, made great play of his raw hatred of hippies. While promoting *Antichrist Superstar*, Marilyn Manson would compare the album with the impact the Manson massacre had on the Summer of Love. 'I think it is [having that effect], and will continue to do that. The media and politicians really made Charles Manson the scapegoat for a whole generation, and I see that tag being placed on me. And it's a tag I've almost accepted with *Antichrist Superstar*.'

Many of the celebrants at the 8/8/88 Rally shared his belief that Charles Manson is 'a gifted philosopher'. But just what is his 'philosophy'? The few members of the Family that remain faithful to their stubby messiah describe it as 'ATWA': Air, Trees, Water, Animals. At one level this is just radical environmentalism, given a sinister edge by its implicit assumption that man is worth no more, and often less, than the creatures around him.

Some radical right-wingers see Charlie as a kind of racist mystic – notably James N. Mason, ejected from the American Nazi Party for his belief that Manson was the spiritual successor to Adolf Hitler. This aspect of Manson's 'philosophy' relates to the theory known as 'Helter Skelter': cobbled together from aspects of racism, biblical prophecy and Beatles lyrics, it predicted black militants would overrun the white Establishment, but would in turn be conquered by another enlightened power in the form of Charlie and his 'dune buggy attack battalion'. Certainly, Charlie has used racist language that is at odds with the hippie ethos, and famously carved a swastika into his forehead during trial – an affectation soon adopted by his 'disciples'. Apologists point out, however, that Charlie's racist rhetoric is what you might expect from someone brought up in the jailhouse, where progressive ideas about racial harmony are a rare luxury, and that the swastika is not just a Nazi insignia but an ancient Hindu religious symbol (with the symbol being reversed).

The most compelling aspect of Charlie Manson's philosophy is the idea of himself as a 'mirror man' – a theme that recurs frequently in Marilyn Manson's work, notably in his allusions to 'the Reflecting God'. At a metaphysical level, Charlie suggests that you deliberately abandon, or even destroy, your own ego in order to get closer to truth or reality. On a more concrete level it describes the source of Charlie's power – his chameleon-like ability to suppress his own ego in order to become what those around him want him to be, whether a Satanist, a hippie, or a Nazi. There are echoes of the mirror man in the singer's description of why he first adopted the Marilyn Manson persona, describing it as 'the perfect story protagonist for a frustrated writer like myself.' The character of Marilyn was designed to be a disdainful misanthrope, a spiteful celebrity who charms his way into the world's affections, but then 'once he wins their confidence, he uses it to destroy them'.

In the words of David Dalton, who nearly fell under Charlie's spell in 1969, 'When you read Manson's words or hear his rants you cannot help but be struck by their obvious truth. Many things he says are not only absolutely right they are profound observations on our culture. And as long as we remain a hypocritical selfish society they will continue to be telling criticisms. The disorientating thing about Manson's vision is that his train of thought follows a form of Möbius logic where every insight turns in on itself with vicious introspection. He'd be really dangerous if he weren't plagued by his own warped mental aberrations.'

Less philosophically, the real reason why Charlie Manson is such an icon for so many of the marginalised and disaffected in today's society is his status as 'king of serial killers'. It's an ironic achievement: Charlie is only known to have directly committed one murder, and might not even be guilty of that. Both his criminal conviction and his notoriety rest on the charge that he masterminded the series of killings he sent his 'Family' to perpetrate. In his defence, Charlie compared his own situation to that of President Nixon sending young American recruits out to die in Vietnam.

Ultimately, the reason Charlie Manson's name continues to feature prominently in serial killer studies is more to do with the media and entertainment world than with criminology. The media reinvents serial killers as mythical monsters, giving them titles more suited to *American Gladiators* or Marvel superheroes than murderous inadequates. Winning him a good deal more fame than the standard fifteen minutes, Charles Manson's status as a serial killer has more to do with his 'star quality' than any particular aspect of his crimes.

Ironically, in a culture obsessed with fame, the condemnatory attention lavished on these murderous misfits may actually encourage them – serial killers enjoy their stardom. As criminology expert Paul A. Woods commented to me, 'No matter how well these guys have covered their tracks over the years, they need to stake a claim on some squalid little footnote in history. Like John Wayne Gacy, who pleaded innocence most of the way up until his execution, all the while selling his kitschy clown paintings to people who regarded him as "the killer clown".'

And like all stars, serial killers have their public. From the respectable retired colonels who join societies dedicated to Jack the Ripper, to the young rock chicks who

HIPPIE HALLOWEEN

Nothing could have cemented the conceptual relationship between Marilyn Manson and Charlie Manson as powerfully as the location for recording the band's debut album – 10050 Cielo Drive, where the Tate massacre took place. The circumstances gave the album's title, *Portrait of an American Family*, just the right sinister overtones. Marilyn himself was able to fulfil his ambition to enter the murder site after producer Trent Reznor rented the former Polanski-Tate house, equipping it as a studio to record Nine Inch Nails' classic *The Downward Spiral*.

Many Nine Inch Nails fans speculated that those songs from the album dealing with murder were inspired by the Manson slaughter. Reznor was adamant this was not the case. 'I had the song "Piggy" written long before it was ever known that I would be in that house,' he pleaded. '"March of the Pigs" has nothing to do with the Tate murders or anything like that. When I rented the place I didn't even realise it was that house. When I found out I thought it was kind of interesting. I didn't think "Oh, it'll be spooky to tell people that . . ." I don't idolise Charles Manson, and I don't condone murdering people because you're a fucked-up hippie trying to make a statement. But it's an interesting little chapter in American history that it was cool to be a part of.'

The atmosphere soon began to take its toll. 'The first night was terrifying,' Reznor confessed. 'By then, I knew all about the place; I'd read all the books about the Manson murders. So I walked in the place at night and everything was dark, and I was like, "Holy Jesus that's where it happened." Scary. I jumped a mile at every sound – even if it was an owl. I woke up in the middle of the night and there was a coyote looking in the window at me. I thought, "I'm not gonna make it."'

'If you thought about what happened there, it was disturbing late at night,' conceded Marilyn Manson, 'but it wasn't exactly a haunted house. No rattling chains or anything, but it did bring across some darkness on the record.' Inevitably, perhaps, a few odd manifestations interrupted the recording of both *Portrait of an American Family* and *The Downward Spiral*. According to Manson, during the recording of the song 'Wrapped in Plastic' a sample of Charles Manson saying, 'Why are the kids doin' what they're doin', why did the child reach out and kill his mom and dad?' kept erupting inexplicably onto the tapes.

'But after about a month I realised that if there's any vibe up there at all, it's one of sadness,' said Reznor. 'It's not like spooky ghosts fucking with you or anything – although we did have a million electrical disturbances. Things that shouldn't have happened did happen. Eventually we'd just joke about it: "Oh, Sharon must be here. The fucking tape machine just shut down."'

BLOOD AND CELLULOID

The serial killer first became a cultural icon via the cinema. In Alfred Hitchcock's 1960 classic *Psycho*, the 'hero' was Norman Bates: a nice, polite young man who just happens to kill people at the behest of his dead mother. After Norman, the serial killer was ready to replace the vampire and the werewolf as the kingpin of celluloid terror.

The 'stalk and slash' flicks that started in the 1970s – notably *Halloween* (1978), *Friday the 13th* (1980), *A Nightmare on Elm Street* (1984) – were an increasingly formulaic sub-genre of the horror movie, plotless showcases for gore effects. Teenage victims were chased interminably by an unstoppable masked killer, who finally dispatched them in a number of improbably colourful ways. The critics hated them but the most successful spawned countless sequels, their primarily young, male audiences lapping up these shamelessly cheesy bloodfests.

As the fictional serial killers in these films became 'heroes', merchandisers jumped in to make a buck out of their youthful fans. The monster-in-human-form became a rebellious icon for thousands of teenagers.

Director Oliver Stone satirised this trend in his savage 1994 film *Natural Born Killers*. Visually overwhelming and curiously cartoonish, many critics accused it of glorifying what it purported to attack. The accusations intensified when some linked the film – which professed to be a statement against violence – with shootings in the US and France. One Texan youth who decapitated a young girl is even claimed to have said he 'wanted to be famous like the Natural Born Killers'.

Trent Reznor of Nine Inch Nails was the natural (born) choice to co-ordinate the soundtrack, a selection of searing noise and twisted rock'n'roll classics that became a best-seller. (Marilyn Manson were due to contribute their cover of 'rock'n'roll Nigger', but Stone opted for the Patti Smith original – though the Manson track 'Cyclops' remains on the soundtrack, if not the soundtrack album.)

The most successful serial killer movie to date is *The Silence of the Lambs* (1991), some considerable distance removed from the stalk-and-slash genre. In some ways, however, it's even more morally dubious than its poverty-stricken predecessors. The maniacs in stalk-and-slash flicks were mostly inarticulate behemoths, hormonal teen frustration personified – serial killer Hannibal Lecter, on the other hand, is a charming, cultured man, a kind of cannibalistic James Bond. If *Halloween*'s Michael Myers is a crude, sadistic wish-fulfilment fantasy for powerless male adolescents, then Lecter plays the same role for mainstream Middle America. His fictional transformation into immoral superman was complete in the novel *Hannibal* in which Lecter not only becomes the hero, but where he even gets the girl.

bombarded Richard 'the Night Stalker' Ramirez with marriage proposals and nude polaroids of themselves, we have developed a twisted, sadomasochistic relationship with our twentieth-century monsters. According to Woods, 'Because these people dig up the blackest impulses from the basement of the human condition, they're expected to be evil geniuses. Hannibal Lecter is an amoral anti-hero – kind of Dracula meets Milton's Lucifer – because we find it difficult to accept some nerdish clerk, or insignificant oddjob man, granting himself a god-like power over life and death.'

Or, as Marilyn Manson observes, 'I look on the serial killers cynically, more tongue-in-cheek. It's basically everybody's fear of death that fascinates them with serial killers. America makes them into heroes. America complains that kids are idolising them, but they don't have anyone to play with.' In a typically ironic comment, he alludes to the parents who leave their children to be brought up by the TV. And, with the media's fascination with violence and murder, that virtual baby-sitter becomes the child's first introduction to the throwaway culture that breeds serial killers.

Shocking as it may be to some, Marilyn's 'tongue-in-cheek' exploration of murderous celebrity is restrained compared to the serial killer trading cards and T-shirts, even serial killer fan clubs, that proliferated in America during the 1990s. Before we join Governor Keating of Oklahoma in lamenting the decline of western civilisation, let's consider the disturbingly articulate – and deeply cynical – opinion of the aptly-named Jim Goad, editor/publisher of *ANSWER Me!*, a magazine of self-professed 'Hate Literature'. In his feature 'Night of a Hundred Mass-Murdering Serial-Killing Stars', Goad gushes that 'Killers are exterminating angels, some of the sweetest souls who ever lived. They are the beautiful people.' If this sounds familiar, note that the article ran in 1992 – four years prior to the release of *Antichrist Superstar*. 'Murder is less of a threat than cigarette smoking, arterial plaque, industrial toxins, or driving a car. Yet people shy away from murder as if there's something *wrong* with it . . . Oblivious to fanciful moralistic constructs, they [killers] have the guts to take matters into their own hands. Are they disturbed? Perhaps, but that's a word we consider synonymous with "visionary". Some would say we've stepped over the line and are glorifying them. Of *course* we are.'

As ever, Goad leaves the reader gasping for breath from the sheer audacity of his assault. He may not be typical of his generation, but Jim Goad represents the furthest extreme of a social current that's been building since the 1960s, a culture of productive hate. Similarly, when Brian Warner invoked Charles Manson, he was invoking a god of hate, just as Marilyn Monroe is the twentieth century's goddess of love (or lust). 'You cannot sedate all the things you hate' is scrawled across Marilyn Manson's debut album, referring to the efforts of our politically-correct culture to legislate the language of hate out of existence.

'They implore you to fight the hate,' writes Jim Goad in *The Redneck Manifesto*, his attack on politically-correct America. 'They want you to kill it, squash it, suffocate it, exterminate it. Blind as bats, they entirely miss the point that the problem isn't hate . . .

It's a natural emotion, not some sinister aberration . . . Hate is as useful as love, and it often works a hell of a lot quicker. Hatespeak is usually more honest than lovespeak, and it's always better than doublespeak . . . How can you protest your oppression (perceived or actual) and sound lovey dovey about it?'

Antichrist Superstar opens with 'The Irresponsible Hate Anthem', faithful Spooky Kids soon taking up its chant of 'We hate love! We love hate!' Asked to justify this, Marilyn explained: 'I don't think people express their hatred enough. They need to let that out. Political correctness has really suppressed hatred. Which in a sense is good. I've got no problem with that. I don't want everyone going around killing each other. That's not my message. But there's no reason to be ashamed to express a natural human feeling, which is hatred. You need balance . . . The word "hate" gets misused a lot, too. People don't appreciate its value.'

Perhaps this is what he's talking about when he compares the impact of *Antichrist Superstar* to that of Charlie Manson's crimes three decades before. Whether it comes from the counterculture – like the hippie Woodstock of 1969 – or from the mainstream – like the corporate Woodstock of 1999 – it pays to be suspicious of anyone trying to sell the doctrine of universal love. The Christian Church sold itself as a creed of universal love, but the actual result was a thousand years of brutality, stagnation and repression. Charlie may not be the philosopher that his misanthropic disciples claim – any more than he's the satanic monster portrayed by the mainstream media – but when he slew the Summer of Love he may well have been doing the world a favour.

'Charles Manson was saying a lot of things that are not unlike what I'm saying today,' observed Marilyn Manson. 'There's a lot of irony in the way things have come into play, there's an irony in the fact that 25 years ago there was the same kind of tensions socially, racially. There was the same threat of war, there was Woodstock, there was a lot of hypocrisy with the hippie culture and their seed of love bullshit. Hippie, short for hypocrite, of course. A lot of people don't want to look into what he had to say, because of what he did, but I think it's important to point out that what he did is really no different than what my father did in Vietnam – my father killed people, he didn't believe in it. Charles Manson killed people, he at least believed in it – that he had a reason for it. Neither one is right or wrong, it just is. Killing is killing, there's no difference. Society makes one person a hero and another person a criminal, it's just a popularity contest. Morality is decided by the man with the most artillery.'

When he became more familiar with fame, Marilyn would revise his view on his notorious namesake, observing in 2000 that he previously hadn't been sure 'who was good and who was bad'. With typical eccentricity, Marilyn maintained he had confused Charles Manson with Doors vocalist Jim Morrison. For the modern Marilyn Manson, Charles Manson was reduced to an emblem of how modern America is just as enchanted with inadequate sociopaths as it is with talented artists. Celebrity and notoriety had become interchangable.

Chapter Two

TOXIC CANDY

When asked to name his influences, Marilyn Manson responded with a typical mixture of the profound and the banal: 'I'm into philosophers like Nietzsche, Freud, Darwin, Crowley, LaVey and Roald Dahl, Dr. Seuss, even the King James Bible.'

Indeed, Reverend Manson of the Church of Satan has expressed his admiration for *The Bible* on more than one occasion, explaining, 'I like it as a book. Just like I like *The Cat In The Hat*.' In comparing Christianity's holy book with a children's fantasy, a brilliant and influential scientist like Charles Darwin with a kids' author, there's serious

FUN AND FEAR

Marilyn Manson is a veteran practical joker, subjecting support bands to his black sense of humour. In the band's early days local amenities were popular targets, particularly those frequented by kids, like toy stores and amusement parks.

One elaborate prank, executed at Christmas, is remembered in some detail in his autobiography. Marilyn cruised the neighbourhood in his girlfriend's car, robbing roadside nativity scenes of their Jesus and black wise man figurines. The plan was to cause a local panic with a ransome note, purportedly from a black militant group, declaring, "We feel that America has falsely illuminated and plasticized the wisdom of the black man with its racist propaganda about his so-called 'white Christmas'."

There are faint echoes, in this harmless Yuletide prank, of the Tate-LeBianca murders – after which, it was suggested that the grotesque graffiti daubed on the walls by the Manson Family were designed to implicate black militants.

HEAD SHRINK

Sigmund Freud was a Jewish physician, born in the Czech Republic (then Moravia) in 1856, whose ideas revolutionised the way we perceive ourselves. The father of psychoanalysis, Freud's theories are no longer well respected in the scientific community, and you're more likely to find Freudians in the English literature department of a university than its psychology faculty. Nevertheless, he was a pioneer in understanding the human mind. Freud introduced the concept of the 'unconscious', suggesting we are not aware of much of what's going on in our heads, and that many of our mental problems are tangled up in hidden mental processes. Furthermore, he claimed many of our profounder problems are traceable to repressed childhood traumas, and, controversially, that sex preoccupies us to a level which we are unwilling to admit. To access the unconscious, Freud used dream interpretation, symbols, hypnosis and freeform conversations with his patients.

Freud's ideas were far from universally popular. He challenged the idea of childhood innocence, suggesting that we are sexual creatures all the way throughout our development. Even more heretically, his research suggested the ultimate conclusion that religion was nothing more than a mental condition, or even an illness. Since his death from cancer in 1939, his theories have come under increasing attack from those who challenge the scientific validity of his research, and accuse him of substituting inventiveness for logic. Digging around in someone's unconscious can do more harm than good to their mental welfare, and blame for the current plague of counsellors, therapists and other quasi-medical witch-doctors can be laid at Freud's door. His theories have also been controversially misused in recent years by mental health professionals who implant 'recovered memories' in their patients, which they then claim as evidence of childhood abuse. The idea that traumatic memories could be repressed since childhood and later recovered was, of course, instrumental in creating the recent 'satanic child abuse' myth.

intent beneath his provocation. To take us down into the sinister childhood underworld he evokes, we have to be guided by another of the 'philosophers' Marilyn cites – the psychoanalyst Sigmund Freud.

If everyone were to write a 'confessional' as full and frank as *The Long Hard Road Out of Hell*, then the world's Freudian analysts would be out of work in a week (no bad thing). One of Freud's most influential ideas was that all of our adult neuroses can be traced back to childhood traumas, often of a sexual nature. He claimed we often repress these painful episodes, and made a living out of unearthing them from paying customers. Marilyn

Manson does such a good job of digging up his own childhood traumas, it almost seems that he's doctored them so that he makes a little more sense in a Freudian light.

The Long Hard Road Out of Hell opens with a young Brian Warner visiting his grandfather Jack's house in the company of his cousin Chad. The old man's private den is a shrine to perverse, deviant sexuality – a dank place full of ancient condoms, grotesque erotica and repulsive sex aids. In an interview conducted prior to his book, Marilyn located in this experience the reason why his songs featured so many strange childhood motifs.

'When I was twelve,' he explained, 'I got my first exposure to sex because I had a real weird grandfather who had a lot of strange pornography in his basement. You know, I started going through it and I found it, and it was a lot of weird stuff – you know with animals, and you know, stuff that you wouldn't really expect to find in your grandfather's house. And that's how I got introduced to everything, and it gave me a strange outlook.' Significantly, Jack Warner, who his grandson paints in a far from sympathetic light, has his den in the cellar – a location associated with dark, primal desire by many Freudian psychologists. The old man even uses the sound of his model railway to conceal his perverse activities, trains and tunnels being among the most overt Freudian symbols for sex.

In true Freudian style, Marilyn sees sexual significance in many of the apparently innocent elements of his 'very strange childhood'. Speaking of his favourite cartoon shows he recollects, with typical bawdy irreverence, 'I think I first got an erection watching *Scooby Doo*. I had something for Daphne.' Early Marilyn Manson promo literature also featured outrageous doodles of favourite children's characters, such as Scooby Doo, with 'LSD' written over his hallucinogen-addled eyes, and the Cat in the Hat, pornographically enjoying himself with penis in hand. (Placing characters from cartoons and popular juvenile fiction in very 'adult positions' has always been popular in the counterculture – most recently with the pop artist Frank Kozik's posters and record sleeves for bands like punk funsters the Offspring.)

Other important Marilyn Manson motifs are prefigured back in the schoolyard, if not the kindergarten. When the Christian Heritage School he attended banned candy, so little Brian Warner harnessed the lure of the forbidden and became 'a candy pusher'. As he observes in his autobiography, 'I gravitated toward candies that were the most like drugs. Most of them weren't just sweets, they also produced a chemical reaction. They would fizz in your mouth or turn your teeth black.' As an adult he would also confess, 'I'm addicted to sugar I guess. Caramello bars because they are so thick and sugary. They almost make you sick just to eat them.' (Sara Lee Lucas, the one original band member who didn't derive his stage-name from a screen star, took the first half of his name from Sara Lee, the popular American cake manufacturer – merging cynically with Henry Lee Lucas, the white trash killer.)

Just as it sexualises cartoon characters, early Marilyn Manson promo art juxtaposes lollipops and candy canes with hypodermic syringes. The relationship between the candy of childhood and the forbidden 'candy' of drugs pervades our consumer culture: legitimate drug companies are constantly admonished for making their pills look colourful and exciting, in case they are mistaken for sweets by curious young children. The child's lust for candy is evocative of the infantile craving adult junkies have for their 'candy' of choice. Just as drug addicts drift into crime to feed their habits, so many children's first brush with the law results from shoplifting candy at their local store. Like drugs, excessive candy consumption is considered wicked and has numerous health implications.

And, as Marilyn suggests, candy can have effects similar to those caused by drugs: from the short-lived energy rush that comes with excess sugar, through hyperactivity resulting from bright food colourings, to more extreme claims of behavioural effects. (Few are more extreme than the case of 'the Twinky defence', where a civic official named Dan White successfully claimed that his large intake of sweet junk food and soda had affected his judgement, leading to his murder of a colleague and the San Francisco mayor in 1978.) Needless to say, candy features prominently in Marilyn Manson lyrics as a symbol of temptation – such as 'Sweet Tooth', from *Portrait of an American Family*, where a craving for sweets is used as a metaphor for an unhealthy relationship.

Another branch of the Marilyn Manson aesthetic sprang from the seed of religion planted early on in childhood. In a letter written by Charlie Manson to President Ronald Reagan in 1986, he warned, 'Keep projecting what not to do and you make the thought in their brains of what can and will be done.' There are few better examples of this reverse psychology than the young Brian Warner's attraction to music condemned as 'satanic' by his Christian teachers, acclaimed by him as an 'unflappable source of album recommendations'. Such sanctimonious condemnation would later provide the fuel for launching the exuberantly blasphemous Marilyn Manson.

Few symbols of young Brian's growing disenchantment with Christianity are as memorably symbolic – even Freudian – as his early experiences on the stage. Cast as Jesus in a school play at the age of six, the impressionable little thespian had his improvised loincloth ripped away, exposing him, literally, to the scorn of his peers. In one fell swoop, the Christian messiah was revealed to him as human, probably all too human. Perversely, this embarrassing episode prefigures the child's future as a rock star with a messianic, megalomaniac image, also known for dropping his pants on stage. (Observers of the feud between Marilyn and his erstwhile mentor, Trent Reznor, may be intrigued to know that Reznor played Judas on the school stage – though Nine Inch Nails fans may protest that the roles were reversed in adult life.)

In one way or another, all of Marilyn Manson's records have been based on the theme of childhood – even *Mechanical Animals*, which on the surface is about the very

THE PSYCHO CIRCUS

KISS erupted onto the New York rock scene in 1972 as an irredeemably tacky extreme of glam rock, but the band soon exploded out of that ghetto with bombastic energy and populist showmanship. KISS toured tirelessly with a live show featuring screaming guitars and merciless salvos of explosions cascading over the band members, resplendent in black and silver, teetering on enormous platform boots. The whole concept – complete with sinister clown make-up and fire-breathing – owed as much to the circus as it did to rock tradition, and the critics remained resolutely unimpressed. They dismissed KISS as comic-book rockers: the band responded by donating blood for the ink of a best-selling Kiss comic book.

Founder and bassist Gene Simmons summed up the band's attitude when speaking of culture in a *Rolling Stone* interview: 'I think Shakespeare is shit! Absolute shit! He may have been a genius for his time, but I can't relate to that stuff. "Thee" and "Thou": he sounds like a faggot. *Captain America* is classic because he's more entertaining.' Kids could relate to that, and did so in their millions, turning KISS into the biggest band in the US by the late Seventies. The KISS Army devoured countless albums, posters, dolls, and (of course) lunchboxes. The self-appointed arbiters of cool may not have approved of these crass, commercial, demonic showmen, but KISS formed the gateway to the forbidden world of rock excess for a generation of American adolescents. (As attested by Christian anti-rock campaigners, who began preaching that KISS was an acronym for 'Kids In the Service of Satan'.)

One of those adolescents was Brian Warner, whose first record album was *KISS Alive II*, and whose first concert, in 1979, was a KISS gig. The boy became an ardent fan, joining the KISS Army, playing with the toy popgun that accompanied *Love Gun*, and decorating his room with KISS merchandise (including the fondly-remembered KISS lunchbox.)

He wasn't on his own. 'KISS changed my world,' said Trent Reznor. 'It seemed evil and scary – the embodiment of rebelliousness when you're age twelve and starting to get hair on your balls.' As Thurston Moore of proto-grunge legends Sonic Youth confirms: 'Growing up in the suburbs, a few of my friends and I were heavily into KISS.' A recent tribute album featured contributions from artists as diverse as Stevie Wonder, Faith No More, Anthrax and, of course, Nine Inch Nails. 'When we were kids everyone thought Queen and KISS were terrible,' said Reznor. 'Now they're a point of reference.'

'I want lunch boxes and dolls,' Marilyn Manson asserted in an early interview, revealing his cultural roots. 'I don't want to change our style to be accepted by the public, I want the public to change their style. I would have no problem if we became the KISS of the nineties.'

adult world of Hollywood celebrity. While promoting the album, the frontman was asked if he was afraid of fame. 'No,' he responded, 'but this record is about dealing with the alienation of it and how in some ways it makes you feel like an infant. You know, everything is big. When you're a baby everybody wants to look at you and kiss you, sometimes you just have to shit in your pants. And the whole world cleans it up.'

Just as *Antichrist Superstar* was about shedding childhood innocence and vulnerability – evolving from 'the Wormboy' into the monstrous, unfeeling superman – so *Mechanical Animals* is about reversing that process. It is, as one interviewer suggested, a quest for purity. 'That's indeed the case,' its creator concurred. 'Only I try to reach that by going in the opposite direction. The more you go through, the more you can leave behind. It may sound bizarre, but while rooting in the mud pool of life I feel myself getting cleaner bit by bit. I would like to become as pure and immaculate as a child. The boy I once was, but that got stained by life.'

'My Monkey' – the Charlie Manson-inspired ditty Marilyn has identified as the best track on *Portrait of an American Family* – has a twisted nursery-rhyme feel to it. 'There's points where my voice and the child's voice mutate together,' its creator observes, 'and you can't tell who's who. I think that's my favourite part of the record, because it's where I really get to become a child again.'

The most overt reference to childhood on *American Family* never made it to the finished edition. The sleeve was to be decorated with a picture of Brian Warner as a child, photographed naked by his mother. 'The point of putting that there was knowing that people would react and they would be offended and say "Look at this child pornography,"' he explained. 'But it's not and for you to see it as child pornography proves that there's something in your mind and that it's not me being sick, it's you being sick.' However, Nothing Records saw it as needless provocation and vetoed the picture's use.

The public's perceptions of child abuse became a central theme of the follow-up record, *Smells Like Children*. At heart a children's record for adults, the EP is a bitter psychedelic requiem for innocence destroyed. Inevitably, Marilyn Manson's less perceptive critics interpreted it as an endorsement of that very same abuse. As he observed, '*Smells Like Children*, for me, was a bit of a joke because people always assume that things I mention in songs are promoting child-molestation.'

While Freud's work had helped to show that 'the child is father to the man', by the time of his death, in 1939, previously 'seen and not heard' children had become sacred icons of innocence. The 1970s saw the rising prominence of child sexual abuse as a social issue – a disgusting abuse of power that seems to be age-old, only recently forced out of the shadows of social taboo. This was a very ugly can of worms, with many people unwilling to recognise that the vast majority of child abuse took place between family members. During the 1980s, evangelical Christians took advantage of this to promote the myth of a secret conspiracy of Satanists who 'ritually' abused children in the name of the Devil. This comforting myth was not only an outrageous lie, but also darkly ironic inasmuch as the clergy have long been associated with sexual mistreatment of the young.

Nevertheless, parental anxiety – which can often reach irrational levels – combined with sensational news copy to ensure the myth thrived for a decade, until deflated by government reports and general scepticism. Ironically, real Satanists remained largely untouched by this latter day witch-hunt. The chief casualties were persecuted members of paranoid communities, wasted government resources that would have been better spent on apprehending genuine criminals, and, ultimately, the credibility of those who propagated this nonsense.

By 1995, when *Smells Like Children* was released, the myth had largely been discredited. However, Marilyn Manson made heavy use of satanic iconography in their promotional material, which, addressing an incendiary topic such as child abuse, still made for a boldly provocative statement. By this time, proponents of the ritual abuse myth had identified themselves as the 'Believe the Children' lobby. Operating on the level of emotional blackmail – they were 'on the side of children', which inferred that their opponents meant them harm – most of their evidence rested on fantastic testimony gleaned from children in the most dubiously unprofessional interview circumstances. The only credence came from blind faith in the idea that children never lie.

By way of contrast, the genuine satanic position on the controversy was expressed by Anton LaVey, who knew – like Roald Dahl – that children can be cruel, while at the same time deeply approving – like Dr Seuss – of their wonderful flights of fancy. LaVey liked children, referring to them as 'natural magicians' – magic being the art of turning the imaginary into the real, the first qualification for which is a vivid imagination. Marilyn Manson, a keen student of LaVey, observed that 'childhood is a magical time when kids believe things, and if you believe something it will come true for you. That's the thing, adults get so depressed, so jaded because everything is so horrible, that they stop believing in dreams and they don't try and live them out.'

As with his belief in the power of childhood fantasy, so with his love of children's entertainment. 'I've found fantasy television shows to be a great escape. The imagination is something that should be appreciated. That's why I think children are innately magic, because they realise the power of their minds and haven't been de-purified by television.'

The most obvious reference to childhood fears, childhood fantasy and children's entertainment on *Smells Like Children* was the sleeve photo depicting Marilyn Manson resembling the Child Catcher – the villain from the 1968 film *Chitty Chitty Bang Bang* (also alluded to in the EP's 'Shitty Chicken Gang Bang'). *Chitty Chitty Bang Bang* was based on the children's book about a flying car by Ian Fleming, author of the James Bond novels, and was adapted for the screen by Manson favourite Roald Dahl. The Child Catcher is a sinister, repellent creature who lures children using sweets, and can track his quarry by smell (hence the title of the Manson EP) – the distillation of the fears of child and parent alike, the predatory stranger who abducts children for unspeakable purposes.

Robert Helpmann as the Child Catcher, the authentically
creepy villain of Chitty Chitty Bang Bang.

(On 'Organ Grinder', which uses samples from *Chitty Chitty Bang Bang*, Marilyn takes on a persona that is half Child Catcher-half Charlie Manson.)

As Manson explained, 'the Child Catcher in that story *Chitty Chitty Bang Bang* was one of the things that influenced the title of that, because he was a guy whose job was to smell out children, and kidnap them and lock them away, but I was real scared of him when I was a kid. But when I got older, a lot of people told me I look like him. So it kind of, I guess, became part of my personality.' But why identify with such a repellent character? 'I, just like everyone else, love fear. And I especially like the phenomenon of villains in children's movies, and what makes kids scared of them.'

The outrage deliberately generated by Marilyn Manson can, in part, be seen as a reaction to the 'safety culture' that is a feature of life in the 1990s. Cries for ever-greater censorship of entertainment grow ever more shrill, in the mistaken belief that removing violence or immorality from the screen will magically remove it from life. To Marilyn, it's all a red herring compared to the darker *frisson* he used to receive from his beloved world of children's entertainment: 'I watch some stuff today, but stuff today is very watered down. As kids we used to watch some very terrifying stuff, but it was really candy-coated so it was given to us more subversively. Now it's an R-rated movie, and if you're a kid you get to see it that way, but you don't get to see it in G-rated movies. It's a weird way that things have evolved. I'm really into the old stuff. I like to scare little kids. I like little kids, I feel that I still am a little kid, so there's a strange relationship with that'.

If *The Long Hard Road Out of Hell* is to be believed, it is clear that this passion for scaring children is heartfelt. Manson describes visiting Disney World with some friends while tripping on LSD, coming across two twins eating turkey dinner, who he describes as resembling the sinister alien infants from the science fiction movie *Children of the Damned*. The malignant, mischievous Marilyn raised his shades to reveal his mismatched eyes, grinned, then sliced his arm with a razorblade. Unsurprisingly, the two kids dropped their lunch in terror, while their tormentor walked away 'exhilarated by my success, because there's nothing like the feeling of knowing you've made a difference in someone's life, even if that difference is a lifetime of nightmares and a fortune in therapy bills'.

It's another memorably unsettling incident in a book cram-packed with them, seeming so cruel and pointlessly provocative that the reader wonders why the author wants to present himself in such an unattractive light. But the point becomes clearer when considering how hypersensitive the modern world is to the welfare of children, and how Marilyn once observed in an interview that, 'The closest we've ever come to being arrested was having a six-year-old kid in a cage on stage singing one of our songs, at the same time having a naked girl crucified to a cross. The kid was out of line of sight from the girl, but everybody else could see them both. I thought it was a weird little science project without actually breaking the law.'

All of which begs the question as to what the purpose of this 'weird little science project' was. The key lies, perhaps, in his identification with the Child Catcher: 'I went through a lot of things as a kid, so I think that as an adult, I kind of became the things that terrified me as a kid,' Marilyn explains, telling of how he felt he was *becoming* the character from *Chitty Chitty Bang Bang*. It's the same process whereby the young Brian Warner – who was terrified by his teachers at the Christian Heritage School, predicting the imminent arrival of the Antichrist – transformed gradually into the Antichrist Superstar.

It's also the same process that Charlie Manson described as 'getting the fear' – a technique he developed to endure his long stays in reform schools and penal institutions, where authority was imposed by guards and fellow inmates by inducing fear. Charlie knew he had to make use of his wits and charisma. His strategy was to reflect the fear of those around him back at them, to become so confident that their aggression melted into insecurity and fear. When Charlie was released in 1967 he started preaching this doctrine to his eager hippy disciples, and some believe the Tate-LaBianca massacres were actually attempts by Charlie to give 'the fear' to the whole straight Establishment (a strategy that had special resonance to the flower children, as 'getting the fear' was also a term for acid-inspired paranoia).

Similar ideas run through modern satanic doctrine – Satanism in itself being a way of manipulating the fears and inadequacies of modern society. It's the same sentiment expressed in the liner notes to *Portrait of an American Family*, where Marilyn Manson claims that the fears fed to the Spooky Kids 'in your sugary breakfast cereals . . . have hardened in our soft pink bellies'.

The Child Catcher is not the only children's entertainment figure to feature in Marilyn Manson's world. Characters from kids' cartoons that blend fun and fear, like *Scooby Doo*, appear in early graphics and oblique lyrical references. (The van used by the show's heroes is called the Mystery Machine – the closing track on *Portrait of an American Family*, entitled 'Misery Machine', is about journeying down 'Highway 666' to the occult world of black magician Aleister Crowley.)

He also makes frequent references to kids' shows where lurid visuals and surreal plots enter the realms of the hallucinatory and the psychedelic, like Sid and Marty Kroffts' early 1970s Saturday-morning show *Lidsville*. (The Great Hoodoo, the evil wizard from *Lidsville*, features heavily in 'Dope Hat' – a musical exploration of the hazards of LaVeyan showmanship and losing identity, whereby the sorcerer/showman can become trapped into trying to satisfy the expectations of a parasitic audience.) The Kroffts' prolific output of kids' TV during the 1970s has now become cult viewing, particularly the surreal shows which blended live action with huge lurid puppets – like *Lidsville*, with its world filled with hats, or *H.R. Pufnstuf*, an orange dragon in a cowboy outfit.

Marilyn is also enchanted by the subversive undertones of Dr Seuss's *Cat in the Hat*, drawing an unlikely parallel between the title character and Satan. 'The character of the Cat in the Hat is not unlike the character of Willy Wonka,' he explained, 'which is also similar to a character like Antichrist Superstar, who is taking the role of the fallen angel. The Cat in the Hat – he was doing his thing the way he wanted to do it, and he wasn't playing by the rules. Neither was Willy Wonka. The antihero in literature is the one I've always identified with.' *The Cat in the Hat* therefore becomes an icon for productive chaos and playful defiance of authority.

Theodor Seuss Geisel is better known to millions of Americans as Dr Seuss, author and illustrator of *Green Eggs and Ham* and, his greatest creation, *The Cat in the Hat*. Born in 1904 in Massachusetts, of German descent, Seuss' anarchic artistic style and surrealistic plots have made him among the best known and loved children's authors in the world. Described by *Life* magazine as 'a devilish puritan', the 'Dr Seuss' pseudonym was originally invented so he could keep writing for his college newspaper after he was busted for drinking during Prohibition. He began his career using his talents in the advertising industry, illustrating a highly successful bug spray campaign in his distinctive style. As a macabre sideline he manufactured stuffed creatures from his imaginary world, using parts from dead animals to construct them like some kind of *Sesame Street*-Frankenstein.

When Dr Seuss finally turned his hand to writing a children's book in 1937, it was not an immediate success. He approached 27 publishers, all of whom rejected his work as too fantastic and lacking in the solid moral message they demanded, before publishing via an old schoolfriend. Seuss' books *did* carry a moral message, but it was not necessarily one most adults were comfortable with. He preached that the imagination was sacred and should be protected at all costs, and that anarchy or absurdity could be positive things. This instantly connected with children – and, as long as the kids were reading, parents were happy.

Dr Seuss' newfound success was interrupted by the outbreak of war in Europe. His fierce devotion to freedom – and determination to show he was a good American who renounced his German roots – inspired him to become a political cartoonist, urging the US to declare war on the Nazis. When America did enter the war he became a propagandist, working alongside the famous animator Chuck Jones on cartoons starring Private SNAFU (G.I. slang for Situation Normal All Fucked Up). Aimed at ordinary G.I.s, the cartoons used risqué situations and strong language to get their message across. Seuss' opposition to the Nazis was heartfelt, and after the war he described the Hitler Youth – antithesis of his ideals of imagination and liberty – as 'the worst educational crime in the entire history of the world'.

Dr Seuss designed the sets, wrote the lyrics, and collaborated on the script for the 1951 film *The 5,000 Fingers of Dr T*, one of his few flops. The story featured Dr Terwilliger, an evil piano teacher who wants to enslave five hundred children to play his giant piano. Full of familiar Seuss themes, like taking the side of freedom against duty, it was too darkly weird for mainstream audiences. In 1957, however, he published *The Cat in the Hat*, whose creation he described as 'like being lost with a witch in a tunnel of love'. Generations have fallen in love with this surreal fable. 'The Cat in the Hat and Theodor Geisel were one and the same,' said a friend, both being characters who 'delighted in the chaos of life, delighted in the seeming insanity of the world around him because he understood that in the long run, order could be made of that chaos, that you could enjoy it, you could have the thrill of it, become a larger, better person for having experienced it'.

Theodor Geisel aka Dr Seuss on the set of The 5,000 Fingers of Dr T. *with its child star Tommy Rettig.*

Seuss never lost his impish mischief. In his *Dr Seuss ABC Book*, a collection of surreal rhymes designed to teach young children the alphabet, the original subversive entry for 'X' was sadly never used: 'Big X, Little X, XXX, Some day kiddies, You will learn about sex.' Perhaps there's some justification for Marilyn Manson making comparisons between Dr Seuss and *The Bible*. Both are bestsellers – over 400 million Dr Seuss books have been sold to date, and it's estimated that one in four American children receives one as their first book. But, while *The Bible* teaches obedience and repression, Seuss preaches the virtues of liberty and chaos. And while Christianity spent much of the Middle Ages suppressing and monopolising literacy, Dr Seuss has earned the title of 'the man who taught America to read'.

One of the most disturbing aspects of Manson is his exposure of the darkness inherent in childhood fantasies – in the case of *Smells Like Children*, one of the main reference points was the film based upon Roald Dahl's novel *Charlie and the Chocolate Factory*. As he described, 'The glue holding all this together was dialogue from *Willy Wonka and the Chocolate Factory* that had been taken out of context to sound like sexual double entendres.'

DEATH METAL AND DISNEY WORLD

Few American states represent the opposing extremes of American culture so well as Florida, where the young Brian Warner gradually transformed into Marilyn Manson. As a favourite destination of retiring pensioners and tourists, the 'Sunshine State' is also the gateway for the drugs trade from South America, with all of the inner-city crime that it attracts. Disney World opened there in 1971, as a larger-scale version of its parent Disneyland in California. Surprisingly, its architect Walt Disney, is held up as a visionary by members of the Church of Satan because of his creation of controlled environments (like Disney World) where robots and models replace inadequate humans.

Resolutely conservative, not least because of its large elderly population, Florida supports an unexpectedly vibrant music scene. It has become the spiritual home of death metal, the extreme rock style that combines growled vocals, overheated guitars and gore-fixated themes, and also bred the controversial, porn-fixated Miami rappers 2 Live Crew, who Marilyn credits with inspiring him, as a white performer, to come up with an act more subversively offensive than their porn-fixated adult nursery rhymes. Later, musing on the success of his 'science project' in a radio interview, he held Florida's social climate partially responsible. 'I think it's the environment that creates bands like us, because it's so conservative there that there is a need for something like this.'

In fact, the Antichrist Superstar regards *Willy Wonka and the Chocolate Factory* as 'one of the greatest films of all time', recalling watching it 'obsessively while eating bags and bags of candy'. As the title change from the original novel suggests, the cinematic version concentrates more on the fearsome, fun-loving figure of Willy Wonka. The basic story is that a collection of cartoonishly-grotesque children win a competition to take a tour of

Wonka's miraculous chocolate factory, each with the prospect of inheriting it. All of them suffer a sickly sweet death through misadventure, except the hero, Charlie Bucket, who graduates as Wonka's apprentice. It is a delightfully cruel, candy-coated fable about temptation.

Gene Wilder (at rear) in the title role in Willy Wonka and the Chocolate Factory.

'I thought Willy Wonka represented the devil,' confirmed the singing Satanist, 'and I've always been attracted to the bad guy. Why was he the bad guy? Later I realised that it's all according to perspective. If you're standing with the bad guy, then somebody else is the bad guy. But I always thought Willy Wonka represented that dark side, because he lured children with the sweets and things that were forbidden.' It was a role Brian Warner would adopt in the guise of Marilyn Manson, enticing a generation of Spooky Kids toward 'things that were forbidden'.

BLOOD AND CHOCOLATE

A British writer of Norwegian descent, Roald Dahl was moved to creativity by his experiences as a fighter pilot in the Second World War. Sitting alone in the cockpit, waiting to kill or be killed, proved darkly inspirational to Dahl's lively, wicked imagination. After an accident left him badly burnt, ending his airforce career and leaving him prone to chronic pain for the rest of his life, Dahl began writing propaganda before publishing his first collection of short stories after the war. The novel *Sometime Never* followed, describing the end of the world with detached, acidic humour. He later disowned it – according to friends the book was 'Dahl uncensored', revealing too much about its creator.

Dahl became known for his punchy, cynical short stories, often steeped in black humour, sometimes containing a dark moral. One critic accused him of 'morbidity, irresponsible cruelty and macabre realism' – when he brought these aspects to children's fiction, however, Dahl really found his audience. Significantly, he never restrained his grislier instincts for the younger readership, and always took the side of his child protagonist, often an abandoned or mistreated orphan, against a vast, unfriendly world. He remembered how children thought, knew they were not the cherubs that moralists liked to think they were, but little devils who shared his fascination with strangeness and delight in extremes.

'Something that will shock an adult won't shock a child,' commented Dahl on writing for children, 'they'll roar with laughter. You can become as crude as you like, as coarse as you like, almost as cruel as you like, as long as there is a burst of laughter at the same time.' What one critic described as his 'notoriously subversive children's books' made Roald Dahl an internationally famous author – most notably for *Charlie and the Chocolate Factory* and *James and the Giant Peach*.

Dahl's personal life was marred with tragedy – serious illness and untimely death plagued his family – which doubtless coloured his dark view of the world. One of the ways Dahl coped was with his macabre sense of mischief. Once, at a dinner party, he handed around a small object, making sure all the guests had scrutinised it in detail before identifying it as a piece of his hip, removed in a recent operation. 'He liked to shock,' said his daughter Ophelia. 'That was important because he felt life was shocking. He also thought it was too easy to look at all the lovely things in life, though he could do that too, he just didn't think people wanted to read about that.'

Chapter Three

CYBERSPOOKS

*B*y the time the mainstream media first started applying the 'gothic' label to Marilyn Manson, and subjecting the gothic subculture to suspicious scrutiny, the band had recently released *Mechanical Animals* – their least gothic album to date. The event that inspired this unwelcome interest was the massacre at Columbine High School in Littleton near Denver, where a teacher and twelve pupils were shot dead by two fellow students on 20 April 1999. The international press went into a frenzy of scapegoating, determined to lay the blame on someone or something other than the two youths actually responsible – no longer available to take their punishment, having also shot themselves dead.

The face that rose to the fore during this frenzy was that of Marilyn Manson – his striking photo-portrait appearing alongside dozens of features on the tragedy, none of them able to justify his assumed connection beyond noting that the two killers were 'weird', supposedly fans of his, and belonged to the gothic subculture.

Most of this turned out to be untrue (the really frightening thing about the pair was their comparative ordinariness) and such 'reportage' only served to highlight the laziness and ignorance of the mainstream news media, tabloid and serious press alike. Treating the goth-kid culture – of which they had little or no knowledge – with derision and hostility, newsprint journalists were determined to start a witch-hunt.

Black trenchcoats, misquoted Marilyn Manson lyrics and the Internet were woven together to invent an 'evil' subculture that simply didn't exist. A good example of this was a feature entitled 'Violent Sub-World Fed by Sadistic Rock and Films' in the *Daily Telegraph* (the staunchly right-wing UK broadsheet). The by-line writer confidently asserted that 'The trenchcoats worn by the Littleton killers are a recurring theme in the Gothic subculture which has attracted so many American high school children. They symbolise everything from suicidal fantasies to mass murder to Hitler.'

Derek Sweet, a postgraduate student at the University of Denver who had actually made a study of the local gothic subculture, said in the light of the post-Columbine

SWEET DREAMS?

Revelations, the apocalyptic final book of The Bible*, as depicted in a famous series of late-fifteenth-century woodcuts.*

Marilyn Manson has often affirmed his belief in the importance of dreams, declaring them not only a reflection of the waking world but of equal significance. Indeed, he devotes an entire chapter in *The Long Hard Road Out of Hell* to recounting some of his most interesting and suggestive nightmares.

Sigmund Freud, the father of psychoanalysis and an influence on Manson, made much of dreams as a gateway to the unconscious. Occultists too have long been interested in the significance and potential power of dreams (though those sorcerers favoured by Manson – Anton LaVey and Aleister Crowley – are largely silent on the subject).

Most classic gothic literature was born in the realms of sleep: *The Castle of Otranto* was inspired by a nightmare about an ancient castle that author Horace Walpole had in the summer of 1764. *Frankenstein*, the greatest novel of the golden age of gothic, had its origins in a 'hideous phantasm' experienced by its creator Mary Shelley 'with shut eyes but acute vision' in 1816, when she was only eighteen. *Dracula*, the enduring classic of Victorian gothic, began as a bad dream suffered by Irish author Bram Stoker in March of 1890. H. P. Lovecraft, the sickly New Englander who became the most influential gothic writer of the twentieth century, used dreams extensively both as themes and inspiration for his weird tales. In the present day, *The Sandman* – an adult comic book created by English writer Neil Gaiman, popular with the gothic subculture – has as its hero a personification of the dream state.

Marilyn Manson claimed that his most overtly gothic album, *Antichrist Superstar*, had its nativity in a dream, comparing it to the phantasmagoria of monsters and madness found in the climactic book of *The Bible*, 'a dream of John the Apostle's now known as Revelations and taught us as fact'.

witch-hunt that goths are 'not violent, they're not racist, they're not into this whole hate mentality . . . But now this group is really scared and they are angry that they're being alienated and attacked once again just for being different.' The goths simply had to sit on their feelings of persecution and self-righteousness, waiting for the media lynch-mobs, with their minimal attention spans, to get bored and identify a new target.

As outraged as many members of the gothic underground were to find themselves identified with the two killers, when the hysteria diminished some were equally outraged to have had their subculture associated with Marilyn Manson. Whereas some newspapers referred to him as 'the high priest of goth', most goths themselves were too entrenched in the murkier fringes of the underground to accept even an 'Antichrist' superstar like Marilyn. To them, Marilyn Manson were not, and never had been, a gothic band.

Part of this adamant rejection came from inverse snobbery. The goth kids crave obscurity and esoterica, and any band whose albums go platinum can't belong to their counterculture club. However, the gothic aesthetic is far from being solely determined by lack of commercialism – and it's an aesthetic Marilyn Manson has embraced to almost unparalleled success.

The word 'Goth' originates with a Germanic tribe between the third and fifth centuries, who carved kingdoms from the remnants of the dying Roman Empire. Naturally, the Romans were not enamoured of them, and 'gothic' became a term synonymous with 'barbaric' (a similar fate befell the name of the Vandals – another tribe who troubled the Romans). The term was little used until the seventeenth century, returning to popular use to describe a new fashion in eighteenth-century England. At this time the British were beginning to establish their international empire, and began self-consciously comparing themselves to the empire builders of classical Rome. The art, philosophy and culture of the Greeks and Romans of the classical era were generally considered far superior to their counterparts from the Middle Ages or Northern Europe – the latter dismissively referred to as 'gothic'.

However, some nonconformist Englishmen decided they actually rather liked the gothic style found in imposing cathedrals, crumbling castles and ivy-covered abbeys. These edifices might not be as ordered and precise as their classical equivalents, but they were somehow more primal, evocative and romantic. Or, as Horace Walpole famously put it, 'One must have taste to be sensible of the beauties of Grecian architecture, one only wants passions to feel Gothic.'

Walpole, nicknamed 'the Silken Baron' was instrumental in what became known as the gothic revival. Although a member of a distinguished political dynasty, this Member of Parliament preferred to spend his time developing his pride and joy – Strawberry Hill, Walpole's house in Twickenham, carefully designed as a showcase for the gothic style. Strawberry Hill in turn inspired him to write a novel – published in 1764 as *The Castle of Otranto*, billed as a 'new species of romance' aimed at 'men of brighter talents', and adding the subtitle 'A Gothick Story'. And so the gothic novel was born.

The Castle of Otranto was designed to evoke the same atmosphere as gothic architecture – it was a literature of passions. Set in a mythical version of medieval Italy, it is a saga of black treachery, supernatural prophecy and virtue in peril so lurid that even its author was nervous as to the reception 'so wild a tale' might enjoy. It was poorly received by critics of the day, and most modern readers find the novel so comically over-the-top as to be unreadable.

Nevertheless, Walpole's morbid romance was a huge popular success at the time, inspiring a legion of imitators. Prominent among these were Ann Radcliffe ('the great enchantress', whose books typically explained away the supernatural in true *Scooby Doo* style) and Matthew Gregory Lewis (a Member of Parliament nicknamed 'the Monk', after his gothic masterpiece of that name which was withdrawn under threat of prosecution for blasphemy). Moral guardians of the day worried as to the effect such wicked and sensational tales might have, particularly as the main audience for gothic novels was young females. One critic described Lewis' *The Monk* as a 'pernicious effusion of youthful intemperance . . . totally unfit for general consumption'. In a now familiar pattern, the indignation of the sanctimonious only increased the sinful appeal of the material they condemned, and the genre became so popular that Jane Austen felt moved to parody it in her 1818 novel *Northanger Abbey*.

However, by then the fad for gothic romances was in decline, and Charles Maturin's 1820 classic *Melmoth the Wanderer*, steeped in 'the midnight darkness of the soul', is widely regarded as the last entry in the golden age of the gothic novel. Gothic architecture was absorbed into the mainstream, admired for its patriotic quality as a truly English style, rather than for its overtones of romantic ruin and medieval mystery.

Nevertheless, from the gothic revival sprang the roots from which the Victorian ghost story and the modern horror genre were born. The gothic aesthetic has much in common with the decadent ideal of the 1890s, particularly the recognition that decay can be beautiful, and terror just as exhilarating as love. (Bram Stoker's 1897 classic *Dracula* is a brilliant Victorian marriage of the decadent and gothic.) Ironically, while gothic fiction was originally considered extreme, these days the term gothic is applied to something that has a very subtle air of menace or morbidity. Both still imply an unhealthy nostalgia: in the original gothic, it was a fascination with the melodrama and mayhem of the Middle Ages, while modern gothic often conjures the understated Victorian fixation with the funereal.

The modern gothic subculture owes much to these forefathers – however, it owes more to a specifically modern phenomenon every part as shocking to the guardians of decency as the gothic novel had been two centuries before. That phenomenon was punk rock, a youth movement with enough electricity to resurrect the gothic aesthetic in a uniquely twentieth-century manifestation.

FUTURE IMPERFECT

Marilyn Manson once said, 'To me science fiction is just as valid as philosophy.' Certainly, the central concept of *Mechanical Animals* is culled from science fiction, just as futuristic sounds and styles became increasingly evident in the gothic/industrial crossover of the 1990s. The idea of science fiction as something other than escapism has gained ground throughout the twentieth century. While its ability to predict the future has proved notoriously poor ('nothing dates as fast as the future', as one wag put it), the genre has proved a powerful tool in analysing the way we live and the direction in which society is heading.

During the 1980s, technologically-biased 'hard science fiction' writers from the USA – such as Robert A. Heinlein, author of *Stranger in a Strange Land*, Charlie Manson's favourite novel – took credit for assisting in the collapse of the USSR. They believed that their positive, American-patriotic version of the future, where peace was achieved through firepower, encouraged the development of the SDI 'Star Wars' program that the Soviets could not afford to match.

Science fiction's dissenting school has always stood opposed to the Heinleinian tendency they dismiss as fascistic, preferring a darker, more critical vision of the future. In the futuristic gothic style known as cyberpunk, decay and corruption contrast with high technology, as tyrannical corporations are fought by lone anti-heroes in the computer realms of cyberspace. The pre-eminent cyberpunk author was William Gibson, who laid down his 'manifesto' in the preface to the 1988 book *Mirrorshades*. The genre quickly established itself as the new cutting edge of science fiction, as practised by writers like Bruce Sterling and John Shirley, and today inspires big-budget blockbuster movies like *The Matrix* (1999 – featuring Marilyn Manson's 'Rock is Dead' on the soundtrack).

This subversive, dystopian strand of science fiction, opposing the technological utopianism of its more traditional authors, is not a new development. English intellectual Aldous Huxley's 1932 novel *Brave New World* – which, alongside George Orwell's 1949 classic *1984*, stands as science fiction's definitive anti-totalitarian statement – is a Marilyn Manson favourite. Prolific genre author Philip K. Dick, another Manson influence, lived a life almost as strange as his work. During the 1970s, he found that reality had begun dissolving around him. Dick couldn't be sure whether it was the government or some alien influence that was messing with his head – though it was most likely the amphetamine addiction that would later shorten his life. Still, he kept on writing strange, powerful books that reflected his unique inventiveness and escalating paranoia.

HEART OF DARKNESS

New Orleans is the uncontested capital of American gothic, a sultry city whose heart still beats to voodoo drums and whose swamp-sodden bowels still cough up the dead in overgrown cemeteries. Its reputation for violence contrasts with the Mardi Gras, America's most famous celebration of the pleasures of the flesh. The ghosts of buccaneers and cajun cardsharps mingle with the spectres of runaway slaves and pleasure-seeking plantation owners in its evocative streets. Although a Mecca for many American goths, not everybody enjoys its distinctive ambience.

'There's not much to do in New Orleans but abuse yourself,' complains Marilyn Manson who, as confirmed by *The Long Hard Road Out of Hell*, is a master of that particular art. 'There's something dark there that's not agreeable. A lot of people go there to die, and at the time that's probably what I wanted.' While he didn't die, he did record his most gothic album, *Antichrist Superstar*, in a converted New Orleans mortuary.

It's no coincidence that the two most important figures writing in the gothic genre today were born and remain resident in New Orleans, which features prominently in their work. Both are women, both are best known for their erotic vampire fiction, and both occupy a position in the gothic culture as important as any band. The first, the incomparable Poppy Z. Brite, writes decadent tales that are poisonously passionate, too unremittingly gothic, in fact, for many pallets. She calls New Orleans, the setting for many of her tales, 'insane and magical', describing it as 'some dimension unto itself'.

The second author, Anne Rice, has been more successful in penetrating the mainstream with her hugely popular Vampire Chronicles, the ongoing series of novels that began with her undead epic *Interview With the Vampire*. She maintains that 'New Orleans is paradise . . . The twilight sky here is like no place on earth. It is violet and golden. New Orleans has all this lush beauty, like Venice and Rome . . . I always remember the fantastic contrast of New Orleans in my childhood: the romance and gloom. Here were all these great big beautiful houses falling into gloom. If I begin a book elsewhere, my characters end up right back here'.

Marilyn Manson couldn't disagree more, calling the heartland of gothic Americana 'Earth's equivalent of Hell'. 'There's a saying in New Orleans,' he recounts. '"There's two things here: bars and graveyards." But at the same time you can use that to your advantage. You can see how worthwhile life is by being so near the ugliness of it all. And luckily, that's what I managed to do.'

While in every major city today it's possible to find the legend 'Punk's Not Dead' daubed on a toilet wall, as far as purists are concerned punk was a brief explosion. As a movement it erupted suddenly in early 1976, but by the late 1970s punk's ideas and energy had disappeared into a nihilistic haze of smack addiction. Perhaps punk had written its own obituary at birth – a cult of suicidal cynicism whose major statement could only be self-destruction.

In any case, many were tiring of punk's playground politics and the ugliness of its snot-and-sneer attitude, looking for something less nihilistic, more evocative. These bands were initially labelled 'positive punk', but the label never stuck. Instead, noting that the bands were getting darker in both theme and apparel, some journalists began describing these morbid romantics as 'gothic'. There are a number of claimants to coining the gothic musical movement. Siouxsie and the Banshees had been an important early punk band, but had a distinctly unsettling, un-rock'n'roll style that vocalist Siouxsie Sue termed 'gothic'. Siouxsie's visual impact was, perhaps, more important than her musical contribution to the goth culture, as her distinctive image – a dominatrix dressed for a Victorian funeral – became the standard look for the gothic femme.

According to Fred Berger an insider on the early goth scene, the male gothic archetype came from Bauhaus, a group whose 1979 debut, 'Bela Lugosi's Dead', is regarded by many as the first true goth-rock record (they perform this eerily downbeat track in the theatrical opening to the stylish 1983 vampire movie *The Hunger*, starring David Bowie). 'The aesthetic was pretty much set by Bauhaus, who were a very gender-ambiguous group,' said Berger. 'The guys wore makeup and they were pretty, and that carried over to the fashion, which for gothic men was lace, high heels, jewellery, thigh-high boots, fetish clothing. Sometimes skirts, but it wasn't drag. Rozz Williams from Christian Death was gender-bending, but definitely a guy. No drag queen would ever consider these gothic boys to be trannies.'

Daniel Ash of Bauhaus gives an interesting insider's view: 'Within six months of starting, Bauhaus started getting the black-wearing audience and seeing the kids dressing up like us. We used to call them the androgynous space demons. Or the wildebeests.' ('Androgynous space demon' – a term almost tailor-made for Marilyn Manson.)

The delightfully-named Suzan Colon, in her retrospective on 'The Gloom Generation' for *Details* magazine, located the genesis of the goth-rock aesthetic with the provocatively-titled Sex Gang Children: 'For a lot of people who had been in it a few years before, punk no longer resembled what they had originally intended it to be. Goth gave them a chance to establish another platform that was specifically theirs. This new scene attracted the dispossessed, a lot of punks living on welfare, shoplifting. Many of them lived in Brixton in the early eighties because it was cheap. There was one band called Sex Gang Children who dressed in a very similar fashion to Bauhaus and Specimen. A load of us used to hang out with their singer, Andi SexGang. He lived on the top floor of an old Victorian house. We'd go up there for tea, and he'd be in a Chinese

ALICE COOPER – SUPERSTAR

Asked about Marilyn Manson, rock veteran Alice Cooper joked, 'A guy with a girl's name and make-up and does theatrics. I wonder where I've seen that before? It's just shocking.' Many have drawn parallels between the two performers, though Alice has also highlighted some differences: 'The only thing that's probably very, very much different from our approaches to music is the fact that they're industrial and we're pretty hard rock, and at the same time they kind of dabble in the occult thing where we're more just fantasy theatrics.' Marilyn has also paid tribute to Alice while berating him for turning his back on the wilder excesses of his youth, and treating the Alice Cooper persona as merely a role.

In fact, there are a number of striking echoes of Alice Cooper in the career of Marilyn Manson: both had religious upbringings, Marilyn attending a Christian school while Alice's father was a minister; while the elder shock-rocker dismisses the occult of late, during the band's early years he claimed the name Alice Cooper came from the spirit of a witch conjured at a séance; Alice (real name Vince Furnier) has also claimed he chose his alter ego's name because it sounded 'so all-American' – the same basis on which the Marilyn Manson moniker was constructed; in both cases the name Alice Cooper/Marilyn Manson was the name of the band, later becoming more regularly identified with the band's frontman.

Both began their careers under the wing of a highly respected figure on the underground scene. While Marilyn Manson were signed to Trent Reznor's Nothing Records, Alice Cooper were picked up by Frank Zappa's Straight label for their first two, decidedly oddball albums. Both artists were pilloried by the mainstream media for their shock tactics, while pundits on the counterculture attacked their authenticity. Goth purists vocally disowned Marilyn Manson, while hippie rock-bores rejected Alice Cooper, having enough trouble accepting an effeminate Euro-decadent like the otherworldly David Bowie. In truth, Alice Cooper was an all-American decadent, substituting Budweiser and TV for the traditional decadent vices of narcotics and poetry. It was an excess of beer that nearly proved Alice's downfall, almost killing him but also fuelling his most startling material. Like Marilyn Manson, his real talent lay in his ability to send musical postcards back from the furthest, darkest fringes of American pop-culture.

Alice Cooper's more perceptive critics described his spectacularly grotesque stageshow as 'Grand Guignol' – a term also applied to Marilyn Manson – which refers to the Grand Guignol theatre in Paris. Originating in the decadent 1890s, the Grand Guignol specialised in short plays full of grisly murder and mutilation by bloodthirsty madmen – decades before Hollywood considered showing a single drop of blood.

Seminal shock rocker Alice Cooper cradles a beer.

robe with black eye makeup on and his hair all done up, playing Edith Piaf albums with fifteen TVs turned on. We had this vision of him as Count Visigoth in his tower, holding court. At the time, [journalist] Dave Dorrell heard us calling Andi "Count Visigoth" and his followers "goths", so that's what he called everyone in the scene.'

In the summer of 1982 a nightclub named the Batcave opened in London, forming a spiritual homeland for the new movement, and the gothic subculture was born – a youth movement with a vague decadent philosophy, gloomy musical style and, most importantly, theatrically-androgynous, morbidly-grandiose fashion sense. The archetypal goth bands came to prominence in the early Eighties. Perhaps the most important were the Sisters of Mercy, whose distinctively ethereal, dark, danceable rock became the seductive sound of 1980s goth. Led by Andrew Eldritch, the band's name was deliberately ambivalent, suggesting both nuns and whores.

Disagreements between Eldritch and fellow band-members guitarist Wayne Hussey and bassist Craig Adams led the latter pair to found the Mission in 1985. The same year saw the release of the debut EP by Fields of the Nephilim, a band who blended gothic rock with a spaghetti western aesthetic. (Lead singer Carl McCoy's lyrics also betrayed a thorough grounding in the occult doctrines of Aleister Crowley, as Marilyn Manson later would.)

All of the classic goth bands of the 1980s cultivated an ambivalent relationship with press and public – not least because (with the possible exception of the Fields of the Nephilim) they were very dismissive of the 'gothic' tag itself. Gothic fandom in turn started to turn its back on the bands that were taking goth away from its androgynous, melodramatic roots toward a heavier, more rock-based direction. By 1990, the original gothic rock scene had burnt itself out. Like the gothic revival of the 1700s, it only ever achieved widespread recognition in its English birthplace and most foreign goth bands seldom progressed beyond aping the genre's Brit pioneers.

Across the Atlantic, the goth label went largely unrecognised, the term 'death-rock' coined instead to describe the macabre rock bands that surfaced from the rubble of punk's creative disintegration in 1979. Typically, US death-rock bands had a more raucous, tongue-in-cheek approach to their subject, referring to cheesy 1950s horror movies rather than the atmospheric classics of the 1920s and Thirties, and shamelessly name-checking Satan. The archetypal death-rock bands were East Coast punk legends the Misfits (named after Marilyn Monroe's downbeat 1961 swansong movie) and West Coast shock-rockers 45 Grave – though perhaps the most traditionally gothic were the eccentric, bewilderingly eclectic Christian Death.

During the early 1990s the gothic subculture began to spread its wings across the Western World, from California to Krakow, though in the process it seemed to lose much of its energy and direction. The classic goth bands of the previous decade were breaking up or entering long periods of inactivity, while those emerging in their wake were depressingly derivative. New blood was needed. This came from an unexpected source that would ultimately provide Marilyn Manson with their first musical feast – the 'industrial scene', a subculture with a history even stranger and more twisted than that of the goths.

In the early days, the industrial subculture's foundations were laid by artists too radical to fit into the ultimately-constricting punk straitjacket. The definitive document on the original industrial scene is Re/Search's *Industrial Culture Handbook*. Written in 1983, journalist Jon Savage's introduction observes, 'Merely to think in terms of "industrial" is, of course, to admit that a particular phase of activity has passed into the history books.' By as early as 1977, Savage had felt the need for a fresh musical form. 'Punk, by this time, had not gone far enough: its style had become a pose: window dressing for packaging and consumption through the usual channels.' Savage and his colleagues on the British music paper *Sounds* came up with a label for those performers they felt capable of taking up the challenge: 'New Musick' – a deliberate echo of black magician Aleister Crowley's idiosyncratic spelling of 'magick'.

While the label 'New Musick' was no more widely accepted than 'positive punk', its concept perfectly encapsulated contemporary industrial culture: modern man needed a musical style to accompany modern existence. The organic musical forms inherited from our ancestors, who lived largely rural lives predominated by natural rhythms, were not relevant any more. The modern urban environment – regulated by mechanical clocks and insistent electronic blurts and bleeps – should be represented in the music we hear. Orthodox contemporary music was designed to lull the listener – something was needed to wake modern man up to his environment and the reality of his situation.

Industrial culture originally represented an artistic movement rather than a youth subculture or musical style. Jon Savage lists five main attributes to describe the industrial pioneers: 'Organizational autonomy' – industrial artists avoided the established commercial avenues for promoting their work. 'Access to information' – the primary role of industrial music was disseminating information, not providing entertainment. 'Use of synthesizers and anti-music' – electronic music, though no longer in its infancy, entered a new stage of technological primitivism when embraced by artists who could only afford the cheapest equipment. In creating this harsh new folk music, non-musicians extolled the aesthetic of noise over melody. 'Extra musical elements' – multi-media presentation, including confrontational use of photographic slides or videotape. 'Shock tactics' – the ultimate strategy in waking people out of the trance of their everyday lives.

Pioneering figures in *The Industrial Culture Handbook* included San Franciscan extremist Monte Cazazza, 'the first to make an artists' film about fist-fucking', Boyd Rice, noise pioneer and, later, Church of Satan member (who would also befriend the Reverend Marilyn Manson), and Cabaret Voltaire, the English experimental-electronic dance band. Arguably the most influential figure to appear in the book was Genesis P-Orridge of Throbbing Gristle – a British band dedicated to breaking down preconceptions about music, art, or even reality itself, founding the label Industrial Records in 1976 before the term had any generic meaning.

POSTHUMAN AND HARDWIRED

One of the most significant developments of the 1990s has been the growth of the Internet and its effect on fringe culture. Those with unusual or exotic interests – such as ones associated with Marilyn Manson: Satanism, sexual fetishism and the gothic aesthetic – can now literally network across the world, finding like-minded souls in a safe, anonymous environment.

This undoubtedly helped create a cultural atmosphere where Marilyn Manson could prosper – indeed, as a band they were probably the first to make full use of cyberspace. The web is crawling with Manson sites, and he himself has taken to issuing communiqués to his fans via the 'net.

Meanwhile, Christian groups have also used it to disseminate all kinds of colourfully libellous anti-Manson propaganda – such as statements supposedly signed by teenage attendees stating that underage teenagers had been seen handcuffed on the Manson tour bus, their faces later appearing on 'Missing' notices. Being the subject of dark grapevine rumours and sinister hearsay was one thing, but a co-ordinated campaign based around libellous fictions masquerading as 'signed affidavits' was enough to move an enraged Marilyn to threaten legal action.

Marilyn Manson's attitude to the 'net has changed significantly over the years. Initially, he subscribed to its common dismissal as 'the CB radio of the 1990s', commenting that 'it just seems to be a gossip column for people who have nothing else to do with their lives'. 'The Internet is a very powerful tool,' he later contradicted, 'but right now it's being handled by a lot of fools. And I think us together, Marilyn Manson as a whole, what we all stand for, should be the biggest spider on the web. I think that it will become our web. Not something that uses us, but something that we will control.' In a 1999 statement issued to his fans – after the mainstream media had pilloried both himself and the Internet over the Columbine tragedy – Marilyn was paying tribute to a communications medium still beyond the control of the corporate state, concluding, 'This Internet is your middle finger to the universe, don't let them break it.'

By the turn of the millennium, Manson's conversion to the power of cyberspace was complete. In an international Internet pronouncement to the Spooky Kids in late December 1999, he declared that his website 'will be my only contact with humanity, so I would expect to see me here on a more regular basis and I would expect you to learn with me as we see the changes that are taking place here in the year 2000'.

The site itself hosts links to a selection of other websites that receive the tacit Manson seal of approval – such as 'Disinformation' and 'Smoking Gun', which carry underground articles and suppressed material, as well as

THE FAS

FREAKS

websites for fundamentalist Christian preachers like the Reverend Jerry Falwell and those that satirise his creed, including the Landover Baptist Church. Other sites that appear to be parodies are apparently dead serious, such as God Hates Fags (just as sanctimoniously homophobic as it sounds) and Hell House (a haunted house designed to terrify teens into becoming good Christians). Some test the boundaries of good taste to destruction, like Evil Dave's 'Celebrity Abortion' game (in the which the player can give famous women messy abortions on-line, in crudely explicit graphics – patients include Princess Diana and Monica Lewinsky, the latter aborted by a cigar-shaped device with Bill Clinton's face), or the Stile Project, which features bizarre porn involving very old or very fat people that only gerontophiliacs or chubby-chasers could get off on.

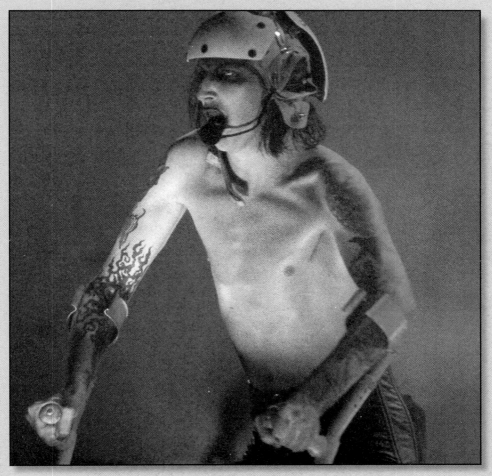

Marilyn Manson takes to the stage as a perverse cross-breed of cyborg and cripple.

ARE 'FRIENDS' ELECTRIC?

Nine Inch Nails were not the first band to cross the boundaries between musical technology and popular accessibility. Trent Reznor has both acclaimed, as an influence, and collaborated with the British musician Gary Numan, who, since he first entered the charts in 1979 with his band Tubeway Army, has been a perennial presence on the fringes of the music scene. Numan took the deliberately sterile, experimental sounds of electronic pioneers like influential German band Kraftwerk, added a melodic pop spin, and introduced the dark science fiction themes inspired by authors like J.G. Ballard (a favourite of Marilyn Manson). Despite popular success Numan was long dismissed by critics, his influence only recently being recognised. Sometime friends of Marilyn Manson, like the Smashing Pumpkins and Hole, have covered Gary Numan tracks, while Marilyn Manson themselves covered the Numan song 'Down in the Park' and his influence, both thematically and musically, is evident on much of *Mechanical Animals*.

Gary Numan and Tubeway Army were labelled 'synth-pop' or 'electro-pop' for their heavy use of synthesisers in otherwise traditionally danceable pop music. Other pioneers of the genre included Soft Cell, who created dance tunes warped with decadence, and whose lead singer Marc Almond, like Manson, later became a member of the Church of Satan. The Eurythmics were another UK band initially at the forefront of the synth-pop genre. Their first success was the 1983 hit 'Sweet Dreams', which provided Marilyn Manson with their own first major hit thirteen years later. The following year the Eurythmics released *1984*, a musical soundtrack to film director Michael Radford's adaptation of George Orwell's dystopian futuristic vision, re-enforcing the links between synth-pop and pessimistic science fiction.

Throbbing Gristle are among the most shocking artists in a book filled with transgressive performers. P-Orridge describes some of the cultural outrages undertaken with collaborators Cosey Fanni Tuti and Peter 'Sleazy' Christopherson, in the Coum Transmissions project which operated between 1969-76: 'In Amsterdam we did a performance in the red-light district. The people in the theatre asked, "What kind of lighting do you want?" and we said, "Oh, just put on all the red lights." Then we played tapes of Charles Manson's LP, *Lie*, cut-up with soundtracks of trains going through thunderstorms, and we went through all different kinds of fetishes. Sleazy cut his throat and had to do a kind of a tourniquet on his throat, and Cosey and I did this thing of spitting at each other and then licking all the spit off, and then licking each other's genitals, and then having sexual intercourse while her hair was set on fire with candles.

There was an audience of around 2,000 people.

'And each day it got heavier, so that on Easter Sunday I was crucified on a wooden cross, whipped with two bullwhips, covered in human vomit and chicken wings and chicken legs, while I had to hold burning torches – people in the audience could hear the skin burning on my hands. And then I urinated down Cosey's legs while she stuck a lighted candle up her vagina, so there were flames coming out of her vagina. Just everyday ways of avoiding the commercials on television . . .'

It would be intriguing to know what the Christian activists so outraged by Marilyn Manson's stageshow would have made of all of this. It's also interesting to note the thematic resemblance between P-Orridge's performance-art and the Manson stadium-rock show two decades later. Spitting, self-mutilation, sadomasochism, sexual exhibitionism, the music of Charlie Manson, blasphemous imitation of the messiah, even parts of chicken carcasses on stage: Coum Transmissions may have been notably more extreme, but they were clearly swimming in the same dark current as Marilyn Manson's Dead to the World tour.

Throbbing Gristle broke up in the summer of 1981, by which time many purists regarded the industrial movement as in terminal decline. (P-Orridge went on to found Thee Temple ov Psycick Youth, whose musical arm Psychic TV despite the capacity to be radically experimental on occasions, were largely to blame for pioneering Europe's acid-house culture.) However, even if the extremists in the avant-garde were abandoning industrial music, others saw potential in the form. Chief among them were Skinny Puppy, a Vancouver-based band formed in 1982, whose caustic electronic atmospheres and tortured electro-beats attracted connoisseurs of cutting-edge musical carnage.

Among these was a Cuban-born musician named Alain Jourgensen, who, as well as collaborating with Skinny Puppy, formed his own band, Ministry. After a lamentably toothless 1983 debut album (Jourgensen later joked that 'we sold out before we even started'), Ministry went on to take industrial music down more accessible roads, appealing aggressively to a less art-bound audience. Jourgensen bolted driving guitars and sampled rage onto the side of the brutal engine of industrial noise developed by crude avant-garde 'metal bashers' like SPK and Test Department. The result was Ministry – piercing without being impenetrable, transferring personal angst into a searing sound that was not only listenable, but almost catchy. On the verge of achieving that impossible act of juggling commercial success and counter-cultural credibility with *Psalm 69*, their 1992 breakthrough album, Ministry hit a creative plateau. However, a lifestyle as punishing as his music seems to have left the remarkable Mr Jourgensen languishing in a field he once led.

Trent Reznor's Nine Inch Nails once lived in the shadow of the mighty Ministry, but as the 1990s progressed the roles were reversed. Reznor proved more than capable of performing the juggling act of success and credibility that Jourgensen ultimately fumbled. Significantly, commercial success for Nine Inch Nails brought rock media awards in both

IF IT AIN'T BROKEN . . .

Born in 1965, Trent Reznor made the improbable journey from a Pennsylvania farm to the cutting edge of popular culture via his musical project, Nine Inch Nails. As an artist, Reznor emerged from the Cleveland electronic music scene before forming Nine Inch Nails in 1989. He was one of a number of musicians then discovering the potential of new musical technology, giving dominance to one creative voice instead of the traditional band format of music as a communal effort. While collaborators have come and gone over the years, in the studio Nine Inch Nails has always been largely a one-man-band.

The highly personal medium offered by electronic music proved perfect for Reznor's approach, a deeply introspective journey through rage and desolation. Somewhat to his surprise, this personal catharsis chimed with a large number of young fans, identifying with Reznor's angst to an occasionally worrying degree.

Nine Inch Nails' 1989 debut *Pretty Hate Machine* is comparatively restrained, an angry electronic dance album with a bitter edge – though Reznor really cuts loose on the album's most popular track, 'Head Like a Hole'. From thereon in, Nine Inch Nails became a musical howl of despair, the sound thicker, more abrasive. *Broken* followed after four years locked in dispute with his record label, Reznor's frustration becoming tangible in a claustrophobic gallery of black soundscapes. (*Fixed*, the companion piece, let a number of Reznor's industrial and experimental contemporaries loose on the album's core material.)

The Downward Spiral, released in 1994, is regarded by many as the definitive Nine Inch Nails album, silencing most of Reznor's critics with a combination of technical virtuosity and raw emotion. Some hail it as a revolutionary recording that changed the face of modern music. (Like *Broken*, it was followed by a companion album of remixes, entitled *Further Down the Downward Spiral*.) The latest Nine Inch Nails double album, *Fragile* (1999), has been described by Reznor as 'Tom Waits on a bayou filtered through a funk blender and slowed down.' It debuted in America's billboard charts at number one, and secured Reznor the prestigious cover of *Rolling Stone* (an accolade which Marilyn had already secured – much to his delight – two years previously), the paper describing *Fragile* as 'a delicate and brutal masterpiece'.

The cultural status of Trent Reznor is evident from his involvement in a wide variety of projects, such as compiling soundtracks for Oliver Stone's *Natural Born Killers* (1994) and David Lynch's acclaimed *Lost Highway* (1997), to groundbreaking computer games like Quake. Reznor can also take credit for launching the career of Marilyn Manson – though all parties now regard the relationship with ambivalence. Reznor, in his role as producer, rescued Manson's debut by giving it the raw edge it lacked in its original form. The relationship climaxed and began to career towards collapse with *Antichrist Superstar*, after which Marilyn recognised the need to get out of Reznor's dominating shadow. The follow-up, *Mechanical Animals*, finally buried the press's 'Eight Inch Nails' jibes by dispensing with Reznor's production services, layered with the polish that had previously been rejected on *Portrait of an American Family*.

Trent Reznor, who formed a musical bridge between industrial sounds and the gothic aesthetic with his project Nine Inch Nails.

Some ugly parallels developed between Nine Inch Nails' very public feud with their label, TVT, and Marilyn Manson's high profile falling-out with Reznor's Nothing Records. Oedipal overtones aside, more than one insider has observed how the relationship between Reznor and Marilyn was mutually beneficial. While Manson learned from the single-minded discipline of his producer, Reznor enjoyed his protégé's talent for spontaneous chaos. Both, of course, are showmen, bringing spectacle back to the musical arena in defiance of self-consciously drab trends like grunge. As Reznor observed of the Nine Inch Nails roadshow, in a comment that could have as easily sprang from Marilyn Manson's lips, 'I'm not trying to hide, or make up for a lack of songs, but essentially Nine Inch Nails are theatre. What we do is closer to Alice Cooper than Pearl Jam.'

dance and hard rock categories – Reznor's great alchemical trick being to create a barbed musical bouquet of truly danceable depression, heavy metal disco if you will.

Reznor, who knows his counter-cultural roots, has shown some ambivalence towards the 'industrial' label. 'There's a scene that's been flourishing for the past five years or more,' he observed in the mid-Nineties. 'Underground, club-orientated danceable music has been labelled "industrial" due to the lack of coming up with a new name. What was originally called industrial music was about twenty years ago, Throbbing Gristle and Test Dept. We have very little to do with it other than there is noise in my music and there is noise in theirs. I'm working in the context of a pop song structure whereas those bands didn't. And because someone didn't come up with a new name that separates those two somewhat unrelated genres, it tends to irritate all the old-school fans waving their flags of alternativeness and obscurity. So, I'd say I've borrowed from certain styles and bands like that. And maybe by making it more accessible it's less exclusive.'

Still, the Nine Inch Nails maestro fulfils many of the five qualifications laid down by Jon Savage in *The Industrial Culture Handbook* – not least the use of videos as an integral part of a band's performance. The success of Nine Inch Nails shows how the industrial shock troops of the 1970s won an entirely different cultural war to the one they believed they were fighting, via the industrial aesthetic's two-decade absorption from the outer reaches of popular culture into its very heart. The electronic beats that once seemed so radical and alien now pump monotonously from techno clubs, playgrounds of choice for some of the modern world's least rebellious youth.

If Trent Reznor's roots were in industrial music, his visual style was resonant of classic goth. This is a symptom of interbreeding between the two subcultures during the 1990s: though they might appear diametrically opposed, goth's preoccupation with melancholic nostalgia and the industrial tendency toward futurism collide in their pessimism, whether an exquisitely nightmarish version of yesterday or tomorrow.

There are also pragmatic reasons why goth-rock and industrial music fell into bed together. In towns that can only support one alternative club, the two subcultures were bound to find themselves sharing venues. Aesthetically, industrial culture can appear a little drab, in need of some morbid gothic glamour. Musically, the goth scene had been snubbed by many of the seminal bands of the 1980s, vocal in their desire to be seen as 'rock' bands – it was a logical step, therefore, for 1990s goth bands to move in the other direction, adopting a sound that was less organic, more electronic. This musical crossbreed is now often described as darkwave, and the cutting edge of the gothic scene today is increasingly dominated by bands sounding more like Cabaret Voltaire or Psychic TV than Bauhaus or the Sisters of Mercy.

Marilyn Manson's success erupted from the bubbling cauldron of gothic-industrial interbreeding. Their sound – until the very public, acrimonious divorce from Reznor as producer – had industrial fingerprints all over it. It was also gothic, though in a self-consciously camp fashion, striking sinister chords more at home in an episode of *Scooby Doo* than accompanying an R-rated horror movie. When asked about the gothic tag, however, their theatrical frontman conceded he'd always liked the genre but that 'I don't think I ever wanted to be limited to that'.

Underground cultists will always have problems with artists who produce platinum records. While living among denizens of the gothic subculture in Marilyn Manson's early years, their leader never really seemed to belong, and would write about the goths with characteristic cynicism in his autobiography. He also describes a later meeting with Daniel Ash, guitarist with the recently-reformed Bauhaus, original pioneers of the gothic rock scene. The conversation began well, with Ash and Manson professing mutual admiration and even talking of possible collaboration, before a sudden chill entered the air. According to Marilyn, the Bauhaus guitarist's friendliness turned to hostility, apparently because this erstwhile idol had taken monstrous rumours about the Satanist superstar's total moral bankruptcy as gospel. Dismayed, Manson concluded that Ash was a 'total schizo, and another idol forever shattered'.

Marilyn Manson may have begun their career with a drum machine (still, at that time, a musical *faux pas* in most genres except dance and goth) but didn't get anywhere until they recruited a human percussionist. At heart, Manson have always been a rock band – a sin most committed goths of the 1990s had trouble forgiving, associating rock with all of the machismo and coarseness they abhor.

So Marilyn Manson have created their own subculture, Spooky Kids, drawn primarily from a new generation where the goth and metal scenes overlap under a large black leather umbrella marked 'alternative'. Meanwhile, gothic purists and Marilyn Manson eye each other with the kind of distaste you usually only expect from an ex-lover. Bauhaus vocalist Pete Murphy took the opportunity of a recent interview with the *LA Times* to complain that 'bands like Marilyn Manson' were getting goth all wrong. Marilyn responded to the barb from the goth pioneer with laughter, claiming, 'I wanted to say to Pete Murphy I'm pretty sure I got it all right and you got it all wrong. Because I have a successful career and you're going bald.'

Chapter Four

DRUGS AND DISEASE

Chapter Nine of *The Long Hard Road Out of Hell* opens with a quote from Aleister Crowley, the twentieth century's foremost black magician. It is his holiest (or unholiest) rule – 'Do what thou wilt shall be the whole of the law.' The chapter is entitled 'Rules', and contains three sets of questionnaires, a spoof of the bargain-basement self-psychoanalysis tests found in tacky magazines. The first is designed to tell if you're a drug addict, and the last question suggests, 'If you make this book into a game and do a line every time drugs are mentioned, then not only are you an addict but you may be dead.'

He's not kidding. Brian Warner may have been a slow starter, not familiarising himself with the world of narcotics until he was nineteen or twenty in a nation where pre-pubescent crack addicts are a growing problem, but once he adopted the mantle of Marilyn Manson he made up for it with a vengeance. The sheer volume and variety of drugs detailed in his autobiography is breathtaking, even by rock'n'roll standards – we witness his initiation into LSD and cocaine, as well as his introduction to others of such exotic practises as smoking human bones and snorting sea monkeys. In classic style, he is destined to crash and burn. The penultimate chapter, which opens with him coming round in a hospital to the words, 'This man is deceased,' covers the near-fatal consequences of Marilyn Manson's plunge into excess.

Fast forward three years, and the album that resulted from his hellish New Orleans drug frenzy, *Antichrist Superstar*, has propelled the band to international fame. Marilyn is on stage at the Big Day Out, Britain's biggest heavy metal event of 1999. A huge sign lights up behind him as he stalks towards the audience, leering like a preacher in predatory mode. The sign says 'DRUGS'. 'I had a dream,' the Reverend Manson announces to the assembled congregation of howling rock fans. 'I was drowning in a sea of liquor, I was washed up on a beach made of cocaine, the sky was made of LSD, the trees were made of marijuana, and God came down from heaven. He asked me to spell

COFFIN NAILS

Cartoon from a seventeenth-century anti-smoking pamphlet depicting the habit as a devil.

'Everybody take drugs and we'll be fine,' Marilyn Manson once announced on a live talk show, but even he has limits. With typical perversity, he takes a stand against tobacco, one of the most widespread legal drugs. 'I don't believe in cigarettes,' he testifies, 'in fact when people smoke, I can't hear what they're saying. I've fine tuned myself to shut out the words of smokers, so I miss out on a lot of conversations.'

But Marilyn does have a point, and he's in good company. In 1604, as the habit was taking hold of the Western world, James I issued a pamphlet attacking tobacco. The royal anti-smoker described the habit as 'a custom loathsome to the eye, hateful to the nose, harmful to the brain, dangerous to the lungs, and the black stinking fume thereof, nearest resembling the horrible Stygian smoke of the pit that is bottomless'. But not even the King of England could prevent the spread of what was the perfect capitalist product. Tobacco is cheap to produce, easily distributed and very habit-forming. Its only minor drawback is a tendency to kill the customer. Even when alcohol, the drug with the longest tradition in Western culture, was banned in the US between 1920–33 on health and moral grounds, tobacco remained on sale.

In a joke as black as a cancer victim's lungs, governments take their revenue and turn a blind eye while tobacco companies continue to make a killing. Corporations make huge profits in the face of all the evidence that, as drugs expert Richard Rudgley puts it, 'tobacco consumption is directly responsible for more deaths than all the other legal and illegal psychoactive substances put together.' It all makes tobacco companies look like the world's biggest drug dealers, while governments resemble the corrupt police who protect them in return for kickbacks. The really crazy part is that, in terms of actual effects, smokers get almost nothing for their money in comparison to virtually every equivalent drug. It's easy to see Marilyn Manson's point when he says, of his tobacco ban on tour, that 'the smoking thing is just common sense, you know. Look what happened with Clinton and his cigar. So I think if you have to have some morality, I believe in not smoking.'

THE ART OF ADDICTION

Marilyn Manson is in little doubt that 'rock and roll is about drugs'. A hundred years or so ago, many people would have said the same about poetry – or perhaps even all of the arts. Many of the Romantic poets were inspired by laudanum, a liquid preparation containing opium. English Romantic Samuel Taylor Coleridge wrote his masterpiece 'Kubla Khan' under the influence of opium, a drug that later ruined his health. His friend Thomas de Quincey became famous in 1820 for the novel *Confessions of an English Opium Eater*, vividly describing his own experiences as a drug addict. The novel was highly regarded by the French Decadents, and indulgence in narcotics became an integral part of their lifestyle. Opium and hashish were still very much associated with the mysterious East, and visiting the squalid opium dens and exclusive hashish clubs that sprung up all over Europe in the nineteenth century was an adventure with the illicit flavour of the Orient.

The most decadent drug of all, however, was absinthe, a powerful alcoholic spirit containing strange herbs supposed to have curious, mind-altering properties. Nicknamed 'the green fairy', few decadent poets did not fall under its spell and numerous poems of the period are dedicated to this legendary liquor. Paul Verlaine wrote, 'For me, my glory is but a humble ephemeral absinthe/ drunk on the sly, with fear of treason/ and if I drink no longer,/ it is for good reason!' Oscar Wilde was of the opinion that 'A glass of absinthe is as poetical as anything in the world. What difference is there between a glass of absinthe and a sunset?' he asked, explaining that, 'After the first glass, you see things as you wish they were. After the second, you see things as they are not. Finally, you see things as they really are, which is the most horrible thing in the world.'

In a familiar pattern, absinthe was officially suppressed at the turn of the century and declared illegal in many countries. But it was not outlawed everywhere, and the green fairy recently entered the world of rock'n'roll when it was served at the 1999 annual awards held by UK heavy metal magazine *Kerrang*! Unable to resist this most notoriously decadent of drinks, Marilyn Manson brought a supply of absinthe back from the Czech capital of Prague in late 1999 (the US having banned the green fairy in 1912). As it says in the punning Marilyn Manson subtitle for the remix of 'I Don't Like the Drugs (But the Drugs Like Me)' – 'Absinthe Makes the Heart Grow Fonder.'

'Absinthe is death' proclaims this anti-absinthe propaganda issued by the French Government in the early-twentieth-century.

DRUG PARANOIA

The escalating 'War on Drugs' waged by governments during the twentieth century, particularly those of the USA and the UK, has been met only by an escalating drug problem. As politicians take an increasingly punitive hard line, so the number of addicts continues to spiral. The failure to eradicate

drugs is unsurprising in view of the near universal pattern of use and abuse throughout human history. Recreational drug use can be traced back to the Stone Age, and it is very difficult to find a single culture that does not indulge in some kind of narcotic. Even the Eskimos, sometimes cited as drug-free, make recourse to a fungi with hypnotic properties.

Another reason for the failure of the War on Drugs is its mammoth hypocrisy. Many young people react with cynicism to lectures on the evils of drugs from politicians with cigars in their mouths, whiskey-swilling clergymen and police officers who can't get going in the morning without a nice strong cup of coffee. As John Strausburgh notes in *The Drug User*, 'President Chester A. Arthur was noted for his love of alcohol and narcotics. Grover Cleveland drank heavily, used ether and cocaine, and his wife, Frances, appeared in ads for a pharmaceutical company. While publicly supporting Prohibition, Warren Harding, and even the supposedly abstemious Herbert Hoover drank bootleg liquor behind closed doors in the White House. John F. Kennedy was rumoured to indulge in occasional recreational drug use, although it's never been substantiated, and he was most certainly a great lover of tobacco. Reagan was given morphine after undergoing colon surgery, and was reported to have enjoyed it.'

The true depth of the Establishment's hypocrisy is breathtaking. While William von Raab, head of US Customs, was insisting, 'This is a war, and anyone who even suggests a tolerant attitude towards drug use should be considered a traitor,' journalists – like Gary Webb, in his acclaimed book *Dark Alliance* – were suggesting links between the CIA and the explosion of crack cocaine on America's streets in the 1980s. Webb claimed that the CIA were, at the very least, turning a blind eye to Nicaraguan Contra rebels who were financing their war by smuggling cocaine to the US.

This was strangely in keeping with the CIA's schizoid attitude to drugs. In the 1950s and early 1960s, their notorious MKULTRA domestic spying and research operation had dosed at least 1,500 military personnel and countless civilians with LSD, MDA and other hallucinogens, often under duress or without the guinea pig's permission. Unsurprisingly, after these revelations, some have seen the Establishment's double-edged attitude toward drugs as symptomatic of a conspiracy. In their book *Acid Dreams: The CIA, LSD, and the Sixties Rebellion*, Martin Lee and Bruce Shlain suggest the CIA deliberately introduced the hippies to acid in order to silence anti-Vietnam War protests. Certainly, many of the foremost figures in the movement made comments to confirm the suspicion.

Beat poet Allen Ginsberg wondered, 'Am I the product of one of the CIA's experiments in mind control? Have they by conscious plan or inadvertent Pandora's box let loose the whole LSD fad on the US and the world?' Acid guru Timothy Leary agreed that 'The LSD movement was started by the CIA. I wouldn't be here without the CIA.' Naturally, many hippies liked to think the CIA's plan had backfired, like Beatle John Lennon who insisted, 'We must remember to thank the CIA and the army for LSD. They invented LSD to control people but what they gave us was freedom.' Others were more cynical, like author and drug icon William S. Burroughs, who observed, 'LSD makes people less competent. You can see their [the CIA's] motivation for turning people on.' His view was given extra credence when the FBI claimed, after Timothy Leary's death, that the hippie high priest had been one of their regular informants on the drug culture.

his name, and I asked him how. He said, "Give me a D, give me an R . . . U . . . G . . . S . . ." What does that spell?'

It's a classic Marilyn Manson provocation, using a mock-Christian revivalist sermon to advocate that great twentieth century taboo, recreational pharmaceuticals, with a sly nod to the declamatory nature of a rockshow's traditional audience-participation section. But is there more to this than gleefully irresponsibility and crude shock tactics?

While few can claim to have done so in such outrageous fashion, Marilyn Manson is certainly not the only person to have linked drugs with religion. Oxford anthropologist and drug expert Richard Rudgley, observes in the introduction to his *Encyclopaedia of Psychoactive Substances* that, 'The recreational use of hallucinogens in our own society would be unthinkable in other cultures who value these kinds of substances as gifts from the gods. Our largely secular use of psychoactive substances is something of an anomaly in the whole scheme of human history and that they could have some sacred function is inconceivable to many people in our society.' In other words, in the great scheme of things, treating drugs as merely a bit of fun rather than a mystical experience is almost an anomaly.

In his introduction to *The Drug User*, John Strausberg suggests that this might be where the West's drug problem begins. 'Some anthropologists and ethnologists believe that modern American culture has difficulties with drugs and alcohol precisely because it has no ritual context with which to control and moderate their use. To the extent that ours is a religious culture, it is mostly Puritan Protestant, with a strong minority presence of Roman Catholicism. It's a tradition that frowns severely on getting high in any way – even getting high within a religious, ritual context, even without the use of drugs.' Priests and holymen in early societies played the role of politicians and lawyers in our own culture, deciding which drugs were acceptable and monitoring their use. Some anthropologists even suggest that early cultures did not develop drugs to explore religion so much as invent religion to explain the psychic properties of drugs.

The English writer Aldous Huxley (author of *Brave New World*, cited by Marilyn Manson as an influence) was a pioneering thinker in this area. He declared that 'the pen is mightier than the sword. But mightier than either the sword or the pen is the pill' in a 1958 article for *The Saturday Evening Post* entitled 'Drugs That Shape Men's Minds'. In this bold feature, Huxley argued that it would benefit Western culture if we were to abandon the idea of drugs as a law and order issue, and return to regarding them as sacred.

'Those,' wrote Huxley, 'who are offended by the idea that the swallowing of a pill may contribute to a genuinely religious experience should remember that all the standard mortifications – fasting, voluntary sleeplessness and self-torture – inflicted upon themselves by the ascetics of every religion for the purpose of acquiring merit, are also, like the mind-changing drugs, powerful devices for altering the chemistry of the body in general and the nervous system in particular . . . That men and women can, by physical and chemical means, transcend themselves in a genuinely spiritual way is something which, to the squeamish idealist, seems rather shocking. But, after all, the drug or the physical exercise is not the cause of the spiritual experience; only its occasion.'

Aldous Huxley certainly used (and enjoyed) psychedelic drugs, notably mescaline – the powerful hallucinogenic drug derived from the peyote cactus used for thousands of years by native Mexican shamen. However, Huxley stressed caution, and his interest in a religion based upon the drug experience was largely theoretical. There were, however, pioneers (perhaps even prophets) prepared to throw caution to the wind. Prominent among these was Aleister Crowley, 'the Great Beast 666', who, legend has it, first introduced Huxley to mescaline in Berlin at the height of the pre-war Nazi era.

Crowley saw himself as the founder of a new religion, called Thelema – or 'Crowleyanity' – which would eclipse Christianity. This most unorthodox of messiahs preached that psychoactive drugs were the (un)holiest of sacraments, second only to sex, and consumed a catalogue of drugs that makes even Marilyn Manson's itinerary of indulgence look modest by comparison. In one of the best known passages in *The Book of the Law*, the bible of Crowley's creed, the faithful are instructed, 'To worship me take wine and strange drugs whereof I will tell my prophet, & be drunk thereof! They shall not harm thee at all. It is a lie, this folly against self.'

However, the Great Beast emphasised that drugs, like sex, were spiritual paths to enlightenment and indulging in them merely for pleasure, or as an idle diversion, was blasphemy in Crowley's eyes. In this light it's difficult to see much common ground between this deviant English mystic, who wanted to 'open the veils of matter', and his modern disciple Marilyn, who just seems to be walking the well-worn path of rock excess. But look more closely at his drug use as described in *The Long Hard Road Out of Hell*, and there are hints that he regards it as more than just a risky recreational pursuit.

Brian Warner's initiation into a form of 'Satanism' coincided with his initiation into the world of narcotics. Both came courtesy of childhood friend John Crowell (a name suggestively similar to Crowley), or, to be precise, his older brother. Crowell's brother was the archetypal white-trash teen Satanist, the kind of guy police might refer to as a 'stoner', and someone whom Anton LaVey would dismiss as an asshole. In Crowell's squalid satanic shrine, the icons are Ozzy Osbourne posters, the religious hymnals are played by Black Sabbath, and the sacred text is the mass-market paperback edition of *The Necronomicon*. The grown-up Brian Warner would later describe the dingy lair as 'exactly what you'd expect from a rural wastoid with a penchant for Satan'.

Most importantly, however, Crowell's unholy sacrament – occupying pride of place on his black altar – was a bong, loaded with marijuana and fortified with Southern Comfort. The young Brian's initiation into teen Satanism and illicit substances climaxes with him passing out. 'Then I threw up. Then I threw up again. And again. But as I knelt doubled over above the toilet, I realised that I had learnt something from the previous night: that I could use black magic to turn the lowly lot life had given me around – to

THE BEAUTY OF THE BEAST

The Great Beast Aleister Crowley

Asked by a fan about the significance of 'the Abbey of Thelema' mentioned in the song 'Misery Machine', Marilyn Manson responded, 'It's something that Aleister Crowley had to do with, if you read any of the stuff that he wrote. A notorious antichrist from the 1800's who died of drug addiction unfortunately. But a great writer.' Crowley was a philosopher and occultist whose influence continues to grow in the present day (not least upon Manson). He remains a controversial figure and even among his growing legions of admirers, there are profound differences of opinion on the nature and significance of this extraordinary man's philosophy. An examination of Crowley's career reveals some interesting parallels with that of Marilyn himself.

Born Edward Alexander Crowley, to an English brewing family in 1875, his poisonously pious parents sent him to a church school where the religious zeal of the teachers was matched only by their brutal discipline. Like Brian Warner a century later, Crowley responded to his religious education by rebelling. His mother responded by dubbing her disobedient son 'the Beast', a name that echoes the Satanic creature in the last book of The Bible who heralds the end of the world. Crowley embraced the insult with pride. He attended Trinity College, Cambridge in 1895, while the Decadent movement was reaching its height in Paris. The young Crowley adopted the lifestyle of the classic Decadent, experimenting enthusiastically with sex and drugs while penning scandalous poetry. But while most Decadents flirted fashionably with the occult, Crowley hurled himself headlong into the black arts as a way of striking back at the Christian faith that blighted his childhood.

He never graduated but began travelling, exploring Eastern religions and investigating the occult lodges that had sprang up all over Europe in the second half of the nineteenth century. In 1904, while on honeymoon with his first wife, Crowley experienced a revelation in Egypt that gave his thus far aimless life a definite direction. He claimed that his Holy Guardian Angel (who some – including, on occasions, Crowley himself – have perceived as Satan) dictated to him *The Book of the Law*. More than a mere magical grimoire, Crowley claimed it was the bible for a new religion that would destroy Christianity. A new aeon was dawning, the Aeon of the Ancient Egyptian war god Horus, when everybody would become attuned to their true selves. And Aleister Crowley, the Great Beast, believed himself the prophet of this new age.

During his life Crowley had few converts to his revolutionary faith, but those who did follow the decadent guru were often talented, influential or powerful individuals in their own right. The Beast was never short of the sexual partners he required for his religion's weird rituals. As far as most people were concerned, however, he was just a colourful cad, dubbed 'the Wickedest Man in the World' by the press but largely forgotten by the time of his death in 1947. Since his death, assessments of his career have varied. He could be monstrously childish, and legends that most of his followers were left insane, financially broke, or in an early grave have their basis firmly in fact – but Crowley was also possessed of a brilliant mind, vast vigour and a magnificent independence it's difficult not to admire (at least from a distance).

There are more converts to Crowley's religion today than there were in his lifetime, mainly in the various modern lodges of the Ordo Templi Orientis, an occult order once headed by the Beast. Increasingly, however, Crowley attracts admirers from outside the occult scene who regard him as a stormtrooper against the last bastions of repressive nineteenth-century Christian morality, a writer whose deviant philosophy, scandalous lifestyle and obscene poetry demonstrate a new way of life.

Like Marilyn Manson, Crowley became a character in one of his own decadent fantasies and refused to recant. Marilyn's description of Crowley as 'a writer' implies that he regards the Great Beast as an artist rather than a prophet, but the following comments suggest an increasing interest in *The Book of the Law*: 'I don't care if something's good or bad or if it's Christian or anti-Christian – I want something that's strong, something that believes in itself' mirrors very strongly, if less extremely, the infamous Crowleyan pronouncement that 'I want none of your faint approval or faint dispraise; I want blasphemy, murder, rape, revolution, anything bad or good, but strong.'

'I think every man and woman is a star,' Marilyn Manson would later claim. 'It's just a matter of realising and becoming it. It's all a matter of willpower.' This is almost pure Crowley, quoting one of his more famous maxims and demonstrating a close familiarity with the Great Beast's work. In turn, Crowley's description of himself following his elevation to the occult rank of 'Ipsissimus' bears much comparison with the way Marilyn Manson looked back upon Brian Warner upon completion of *Antichrist Superstar*. 'I am myself a physical coward,' wrote Crowley with disarming self-abasement, 'but I have exposed myself to every form of disease, accident, and violence; I am dainty and delicate, but I have driven myself to delight in dirty and disgusting debauches, and to devour human excrements and human flesh. I am at this moment defying the power of drugs to disturb my destiny and divert my body from its duty . . .Yet I have mastered every mode of my mind, and made myself a morality more severe than any other in the world if only by virtue of its absolute freedom from any code of conduct.'

attain a position of power that other people would envy and accomplish things that other people couldn't. I also learned that I didn't like smoking pot – or the taste of bongwater.'

This passage may lack the biblical grandeur of Crowley – indeed, the author displays a characteristic decadent tendency to wallow in the sordid – but Marilyn is obviously implying that this experience had some darkly spiritual significance. That implication is even stronger in his description of his first LSD trip in Florida during 1990. Manson doesn't just describe a bad trip but a journey into his own past and future, haunted by ominous portents, the nightmare journey of a pop-culture shaman into his own underworld. He finds himself screwing Nancy, a girl previously dismissed as a psycho, who, in his hallucinatory world, becomes increasingly demonic. 'This is it,' he writes of that moment. 'I'm screwing the devil. I've sold my soul.' While it lacks the formal rites and robes, what Marilyn describes is classic Crowleyan sex magic, a contemporary demonic pact.

Aleister Crowley died in England 1947, still consuming enough heroin to kill a whole squad of guardsmen. It's easy to believe that, had the Great Beast's ghost been haunting the Big Day Out in 1999, he would have given his blessing to Marilyn Manson's brief, blasphemous sermon. It's less certain what Crowley might have made of the song that followed it, 'I Don't Like the Drugs (But the Drugs Like Me)' – as more than one critic has commented, the song is a pithily witty summation of anyone in the thrall of a drug habit.

Crowley's attitude to drugs reflects some of the harshest aspects of his creed, dismissing those not strong enough to conquer addiction as 'slaves' in his *Book of the Law*: 'Pity not the fallen! I never knew them. I am not for them. I console not: I hate the consoled and consoler. I am unique, a conqueror. I am not of the slaves that perish. Be they damned and dead! Amen . . .'

Such sentiments are broadly reflected in Marilyn's own views, his point being that drugs are not the problem – it's the people who use them, suggesting that addicts give purely recreational drug users a bad name. This recurring line – the difference between 'use' and 'abuse' – is a radical statement at a time when orthodox wisdom insists all illicit drug use is automatically 'abuse'. As outlined by Church of Satan High Priest Anton LaVey (himself vehemently anti-drugs) in *The Satanic Bible*, Marilyn Manson's policy is 'Indulgence . . . NOT Compulsion.'

Satanism as a creed worships the flesh and its pleasures, and is almost obliged to exhibit sympathy to sin. But earthly pleasures pursued to excess are rarely pleasurable, and often lead to dependence and self-destruction – blasphemy to a creed that preaches independence and self-empowerment. To address this problem, LaVey emphasised that excessive self-indulgence is merely masochism in a perverse guise. When the Church of Satan was founded in San Francisco during 1966 as 'flower power' was reaching its height, LaVey asserted that those hippies who felt obliged to take drugs to be cool were no freer than the straight folk who avoided drugs to be respectable.

As the decades passed, the Church of Satan's disdain for the hippies advanced into hatred. Whilst none of the Church's central tenets changed, some of them were expressed more aggressively. An article was published in a 1994 edition of *The Black Flame*, the Church of Satan's International Forum, by a Satanist calling himself Azazel, entitled 'Drugs and Natural Selection': 'The government has no right or responsibility to prevent any adult of legal age from consuming any drug, no matter what the personal detriment is. This freedom to choose is a natural human right. Drugs, however, should be neither condoned nor advocated, as they are part of a natural screening process separating the weak from the strong which greatly contributes to natural selection and population control. Overdose, lack of direction, apathy, listlessness, addiction, and all the other wonderful side effects of drugs allow these individuals to be exploited, for by such behaviour they are prey.' Natural selection – the idea that the strong will thrive while the weak will perish – is a dominant force not just in the animal world but in human society, according to believers in Social Darwinism, one of the key tenets of *The Satanic Bible*.

Azazel's opinions reflect those of an increasing number of members within the Church of Satan. Contrary to myths spread by Christian fundamentalists that condemn Satanism as an international drugs cult, the ethos of the CoS was traditionally anti-narcotics. This has caused some recent tension within the movement, since two icons revered by modern members – Aleister Crowley (who LaVey regarded as a 'druggy poseur') and Charlie Manson – both have reputations as habitual drug users. The fact that the highest profile Church of Satan recruit of the 1990s (namely Marilyn Manson) also had a well-known penchant for narcotics caused severe disquiet.

In reality, Marilyn's views are not as far from those of Azazel as they may first appear. In one talkshow discussing drugs, he went so far as to say, 'I think drugs can also work as a bit of Social Darwinism.' Marilyn's speculation is especially bold, when one considers his description in *The Long Hard Road Out of Hell* of how drugs nearly destroyed him during the recording of *Antichrist Superstar*. He explored this paradox whilst interviewed about the recording of *Mechanical Animals*, an album littered with references to drugs.

'The problem with *Antichrist Superstar* was I was put in a position where I was made very unsure of myself. I was questioning everything I did because no one had any confidence in what I was doing and I was taking so many drugs to ease that misery and frustration. It's only when you're in that weak frame of mind that drugs can really hurt you. If you're a competent drug user than there's nothing to fear. No drugs were sought out of depression or confusion this time because I was very sure about what I was doing. They were just sought out of enjoyment or decadence. The record was written on drugs about drugs, and it will likely be performed on drugs as well.'

And what of Aleister Crowley, whose survival to the age of 72 on a suicidal diet of drugs was almost a magical act in itself? He had evangelised tirelessly in favour of narcotic indulgence, writing articles under pseudonyms with titles like 'The Great Drug Delusion' and 'The Drug Panic' and a novel with autobiographical components entitled *Diary of a*

Drug Fiend (echoed, of course, in the Marilyn Manson remix title 'Diary of a Dope Fiend'). Consciously, Crowley almost certainly saw himself as the novel's impressive guru character who the weak and neurotic seek for help, while subconsciously he must have felt something in common with those who needed help for their drug problems.

For even the Great Beast, whose *Book of the Law* reviled addicts as slaves, was forced at times to confess he wasn't wholly free from addiction. Cocaine, a drug generally regarded as psychologically rather than physically addictive, was a favourite of Crowley's (and also of Marilyn Manson's, featuring prominently in *The Long Hard Road Out of Hell*). In his 'magical record', Crowley wrote, 'Why is it that one takes cocaine (but no other drug) gluttonously, dose upon dose, neither feeling the need for it, nor hoping to get any good from it? I have found that every time. Three doses, intelligently taken, secure all one wants. Yet, if the stuff is at hand, it is almost impossible not to go on . . . Why take thirty doses (or is it sixty? I haven't a ghost of a guess) to get into a state neither pleasant nor in any way desirable, but fraught with uneasiness, self-contempt, alarm, discomfort and irritation at the ever present thought of "Hell! Now I have to endure the reaction" while well aware that with three one can get all one wants without one single drawback.' I don't like the drugs (but the drugs like me)! . . .

Asked about his favourite subject at school, Marilyn joked that it was 'health'. It's easy to dismiss this as another throwaway quip, but it's true that health industry pharmaceuticals seem to preoccupy him nearly as much as recreational drugs. *Mechanical Animals*, Marilyn Manson's most overtly drug-themed album, combines images of narcotic excess with those of surgical sterility. The CD even looks like a pill, while its content plays with the idea that the cure may be as bad as the disease.

Medical themes have long haunted Manson's material. Hypodermic syringes – simultaneously medical instruments and symbols of illicit drug abuse – figure heavily in early promotional imagery. Marilyn himself has even taken to the stage dressed in bizarre remedial garb. *Smells Like Children* features 'May Cause Discoloration of the Urine or Faeces', an unsettling sampled phone call by a patient concerned about his medication. Diagrams lifted from anatomical texts are the dominant motif in *The Long Hard Road Out of Hell*. In modern culture, of course, where spirituality has become divorced from drugs, doctors have taken over the traditional shaman's role in deciding which mind-altering drugs are acceptable for use and monitoring their distribution.

The medical profession has become our culture's most prolific drug pusher. Aldous Huxley, who was sympathetic to psychedelic drug experimentation, wrote that, 'In theory, tranquillisers should be given only to persons suffering from rather severe forms of neurosis or psychosis. In practice, unfortunately, many physicians have been carried away by the current pharmacological fashion and are prescribing tranquillisers to all and sundry . . . In the present case, millions of patients who have no real need of the tranquillisers have been given the pills by their doctors and have learnt to resort to them in every predicament, however triflingly uncomfortable.'

This was written in 1958, and few would argue that this pharmacological fashion has not only continued, but progressed to the present point where, as author Elizabeth Wurtzel puts it in her celebrated Generation X book, we all live in the *Prozac Nation*. It is not just rock stars or counter-cultural rebels who turn to drugs to alleviate mild psychological or emotional discomfort – or even just boredom – but our entire culture that seems to be taking to psychoactive substances. Perhaps we always have. As more than one historian has observed, most of the Middle Ages were experienced in an altered state of mind by a population chronically addicted to alcohol. (Which doesn't even allow for those at the fringes of society, labelled witches by their persecutors, who made use of narcotics to commune with their unholy gods.)

Another reason for the hallucinatory aura that hung over Medieval Europe was the widespread malnutrition and disease. Many modern magicians follow Aleister Crowley and make recourse to fasting in order to attune their minds to other dimensions. Marilyn Manson, as a band, made deliberate use of psychological trauma during the recording of *Antichrist Superstar* in order to reach altered states of consciousness. While they never went as far as making themselves deliberately ill, the band's self-conscious, self-destructive self-indulgence invited physical and mental collapse, and it's certainly true that there are parallels between the psychological effects of the drugs some people go to great lengths

THE SPOILS OF WAR

Of all Marilyn Manson's health complications, perhaps the most exotic are the results of his father's military career. As a helicopter pilot during the Vietnam War, Hugh Warner sprayed Agent Orange on the Vietnamese jungles – the most notorious of the highly toxic defoliants used by the US army in the conflict (86 million litres were dropped in all), Agent Orange was designed to deprive the enemy of all cover by killing plant life. The strategy was abandoned in 1970, after disappointing results and mounting popular concern over scientific tests linking the defoliant's chemical properties with cancers and birth defects.

The 1978 film The Deer Hunter *– one of the most powerful statements on the traumatic repercussions of the Vietnam war.*

Campaigns by Vietnam veterans to have their illnesses recognised as side effects of Agent Orange continue to this day. Marilyn Manson recalls how the young Brian Warner was obliged to undergo scientific trials, to determine whether his father's exposure to Agent Orange had resulted in any physical or psychological problems for the boy. 'I don't think there were any,' he observes, 'though my enemies might disagree.'

National humiliation, particularly in war, is one of the factors that plunges a culture into decadence. The decadence of late nineteenth century Paris followed France's crushing defeat by the Germans in the Franco-Prussian War. The decadence of 1920s Berlin is directly linked to Germany's loss of the First World War in 1918. Could there be a link between American decadence – as personified by Marilyn Manson – and the humiliating defeat experienced by the US in Vietnam?

to obtain and the illnesses most of us go to great lengths to avoid. Hallucinations, hyperactivity, even elation, are just some of the sensations that can accompany both sickness and a drug-induced high.

When one journalist commented on Marilyn wearing his pyjamas for an interview, he responded that 'It was a hospital gown, actually, from when I was hospitalised.' Rather than relating the nature of that specific incident, he went into a catalogue of past ailments: 'Well, when I was a child I had pneumonia twice. And I had polyps removed from my rectum. I had to have my urethra enlarged because the hole through which I urinate wasn't large enough to accommodate the stream I was projecting. I had an allergic reaction to antibiotics once and I almost died. Recently, I was hospitalised for depression and scarification. Self-mutilation. And I've had my legs waxed, but I wasn't in the hospital for that.'

To this already long list of illnesses, *The Long Hard Road Out of Hell* adds TMJ syndrome (a dysfunction of the jaw, caused by having his tooth punched out**)** and a heart condition known as Wolff-Parkinson-White syndrome. By high school age, 'Hospitals and bad experiences with women, sexuality and private parts were completely familiar to me,' Manson observes, linking sickness and eroticism in a clinical, fetishised manner.

Watching his often alarmingly physical performances, it's difficult to think of Marilyn Manson as sickly in the conventional sense. But still, disease and medication loom large in his world – possibly because he recognises a universally morbid part of the human condition, the knowledge that disease will end most of our lives while medicine is sometimes the only thing standing in between us and our own mortality. However, it could also be that his excessive, self-indulgent lifestyle has given bad health a very large role in his life.

It's intriguing to note how disease figured so heavily in the lives of the original decadent artists of the nineteenth century. Edgar Allan Poe, the American writer whose work inspired the movement in France, had a delicate constitution made worse by his chronic alcoholism. Unhappy familial and romantic experiences made him associate feminine beauty with the delicate pallor of fatal illness. In turn, his stories and poetry were filled with frail heroes with ancestral ailments, and unspeakably beautiful women on, or past, the brink of death. These archetypes are the seeds from which the delicate, pale-faced aesthetic of the modern gothic subculture grew.

At the height of the Decadent movement, in 1890s Paris, illness was almost a fashion. The Decadents were particularly attracted to the theory of a medical condition known as neurasthenia. According to Brian Stableford, in *Moral Ruins*, his anthology of decadent writing, 'The neurasthenic was a physically weak and over-sensitive individual, likely also to be morally weak, permanently possessed by apathy and spiritual impotence.' If great sensitivity and a touch of evil were the symptom, or even the cause, of a disease – then might not artistic genius also be a pathological condition?

SONNETS OF SYPHILIS AND SATAN

An archetypally decadent devil illustrating Baudelaire's masterpiece The Litanies of Satan.

Born in 1821, the Frenchman Charles Baudelaire is regarded as the first poet of the Decadent movement. Heavily influenced by hard-drinking, melancholic American author Edgar Allan Poe, Baudelaire developed a style of poetry that soared effortlessly between the squalor of the gutter and sublime beauty. He embraced a lifestyle that complimented the decadence of his work, haunting the brothels and absinthe bars of Paris, becoming known for his dandified dress and cynical wit. His masterpiece, a collection of poems entitled *Les Fleurs du mal* (*The Flowers of Evil*), appeared in 1857, and generated an immediate scandal, containing verses of morbid sexuality, ghoulish meditation and odes to Satan. He was successfully prosecuted by the French Government for offending public morals, fined, and had six of the poems officially removed from the collection and banned from reprint.

Baudelaire caught syphilis as a young man, which, in its progressive form, caused him increasing pain throughout his life, leading him to seek comfort in opium and alcohol. His poem 'Voyage to Cytherea' describes visiting an island sacred to the goddess of love, but finding only a rotting corpse hanging from a gibbet whose 'heavy entrails flowed down his thighs'. 'On your isle, O Venus, I found nothing erect but a symbolic gallows, where hung my own image.' Baudelaire's poor health, combined with his licentious lifestyle, condemned him to an early grave in 1867. He is now regarded as one of the greatest, if darkest, poets of the modern age, and in 1949 the ban on his most shocking verses was finally lifted, nearly a century after they were written.

'. . . Would be Decadents were initially prepared to take great pains to cultivate their neurasthenia,' writes Stableford, 'or at the very least to be conscientious hypochondriacs. They treasured their symptoms, not only as reflections of the unfortunate nature of the human condition but also evidences of their superiority over the common herd.' And the sick shall inherit the earth . . .

Chapter Five

CHICKS WITH DICKS

As we enter the new millennium, the gender gap seems to be narrowing. Images of masculine and feminine beauty look increasingly similar. While male film stars, most notably Leonardo DiCaprio, are increasingly androgynous in appearance, their female equivalents seem to be chosen for features and figures reminiscent of an adolescent boy. Voluptuous sex symbols like Marilyn Monroe would have trouble launching their careers in the 1990s, while Mae West, the original blonde bombshell, would never get past the casting couch today. Marilyn Manson, who plays outrageously with sexual ambiguity, can obviously be seen as the next step in this cultural preoccupation with gender bending – but that's only part of the story.

As with drugs, this would appear to be an area where Marilyn Manson is at odds with the philosophies of the Church of Satan and his spiritual mentor, 'Black Pope' Anton LaVey. The Church of Satan was founded in the mid-1960s, around the time modern feminism was undergoing its genesis. LaVey regarded the movement with dismay, seeing it as yet another drab fad that went against aesthetics and nature. While portrayed as a move towards liberation, in LaVey's cosmology feminism was just another aspect of the blurring of gender distinctions that began in the 1960s. Whether it was youth cults like the hippies, with their unisex clothes and long hair, or fashion models like Twiggy, who deliberately fostered a boyish look, the 1960s were characterised by androgyny. And LaVey did not approve.

He saw the real engine behind this trend not as liberty but the pressure to conform. Corporate America wants good consumers, and consumers who all want the same thing are the easiest to satisfy. So homogenisation is actively, if covertly, encouraged, and all marks of difference and distinction, including those of gender, must gradually be eroded. Feminism, as it developed, was not so much a movement celebrating feminine power as an attempt to turn women into second-rate men. Feminists claimed to be seeking equality with men, but, as many post-feminists later came to realise, concepts of sexual equality and sexual individualism are simply incompatible.

The Black Pope's most public counter-blast against feminism came in his 1970 book *The Compleat Witch* (later retitled *The Satanic Witch*), a battle manual for women to use in the war of the sexes. The first chapter finishes with a rule of engagement that LaVey considers so important he puts it in capitals: 'NEVER FORGET THAT YOU ARE A WOMAN, AND THE GREATEST POWERS YOU CAN EMPLOY AS A WITCH ARE TOTALLY DEPENDENT ON YOUR OWN SELF-REALIZATION THAT IN BEING A WOMAN YOU ARE *DIFFERENT* FROM A MAN AND THAT VERY DIFFERENCE MUST BE EXPLOITED.'

LaVey's belief, that men are more potent if masculine and women more powerful if feminine, remains Church of Satan dogma. To the present day, the organisation continues to extol the virtues of the curvaceous, sexually-predatory female, most notably in the work of the pop artist Coop.

Predictably, LaVey was labelled a misogynist – a mantle he willingly accepted, going so far as to publish an essay entitled 'Confessions of a Closet Misogynist' in his 1992 collection *The Devil's Notebook*. As ever with this ingeniously provocative thinker, there was a twist in the tail: LaVey didn't hate women but was in awe of their power, treating them with the blend of suspicion, fear and respect afforded to a worthy foe.

His next collection, the posthumously published *Satan Speaks!*, featured an essay entitled 'On Women or: Why My Right-Hand Man Must Be a Woman', in which he declared, 'I believe woman is the dominant sex, with or without feminist validation.' A change of direction? Not at all. Ever since he first conducted seminars on witchcraft in the early days of the Church of Satan, LaVey always lauded seductive, spirited women as 'Satanists'. After all, it was Eve who tempted Adam with the apple in The Bible, and Adam's oft-forgotten first wife, Lilith, who was ejected from Paradise for her independence and sex drive, fleeing to the wilderness to become Satan's consort.

So where does Marilyn Manson fit into all this?

LaVey never preached against effeminate men or masculine women – indeed, the Church of Satan's early membership was a fabulous freakshow expressing individualism in various unique ways, sometimes transcending boundaries of sexuality and gender. What the Black Pope opposed was the sexual halfway-house promoted in the mainstream media, the unisex ideal of the self-consciously sensitive man and crudely aggressive woman. The sexes, said LaVey, should be different, not equal. However, while he railed against the neutering of gender, stressing that a true individual could never be free of either overt masculine or feminine traits, he never said that you couldn't be *both*.

In the name of embodying opposing extremes, Marilyn Manson highlights powerful icons of voluptuous womanhood and domineering manhood, in Marilyn Monroe and Charlie Manson. His persona combines elements of traditional masculinity – like his aggressive stage performances – with characteristics traditionally associated with femininity, such as his flamboyant dress and make-up. Asked once if he was a transvestite, Marilyn responded that 'a transvestite is a man that dresses like a woman, but I think that

I'm a composite of both male and female. I'm not trying to look like a woman – I'm trying to look like something that is both.' It's a stance that some members of the Church of Satan (including, to an extent, LaVey, who refused to address him as 'Marilyn') were uncomfortable with, but it didn't contradict their central ethos of radical individualism.

Marilyn Manson's incarnation as an extraterrestrial on *Mechanical Animals* was more problematic, from a satanic point-of-view. While previously he had embodied both powerful male and female characteristics, he now seemed to be sailing dangerously close to the sexual no-man's-land LaVey abhorred. Interestingly, his new image was a hybrid of alien and angel – evocative of the medieval religious paintings of Lucifer cast from Heaven by St. Michael, aided by strikingly androgynous angels. While the forces of evil in these paintings have prominent male and female genitals (and often both), their virtuous, desexed foes look almost like angelic shop-window mannequins. Just as the grey aliens of modern myth – which believers hope will save the earth – are sexless, almost featureless in appearance, so the angels our ancestors prayed to for salvation were inhumanly genderless. Marilyn himself claims that *Mechanical Animals* is about Jesus in the same way *Antichrist Superstar* was about Lucifer. It's difficult not to wonder whether he's suggesting the idea of Jesus as a sexually-neutered eunuch messiah, considered holy by his followers but regarded with contempt by sensually-inclined Satanists.

Asked whether his image was becoming more feminine, Marilyn responded, 'More androgynous. At the same time more sexless too – all of the details are stripped. Feminine and vulnerable, I suppose . . . it's about getting completely sexual, completely sexless at the same time.' How his sexless alien-androgyne persona could be considered 'completely sexual' is far from clear.

Like Anton LaVey, Marilyn Manson has subverted accusations of misogyny by declaring himself to have been a misogynist. The most damning evidence is provided by the accused: in *The Long Hard Road Out of Hell*, he recalls how the young Brian Warner would steal money and private notes from girls at the Christian Heritage School, not just for financial reward or information, but also the satisfaction of causing distress among his female targets. He later describes a girl who worked at the local mall who he lusted after, but considered unobtainable, making recourse to what he describes as 'malicious, asinine behaviour' with a series of threatening prank calls. Marilyn admits he was fully aware of the distress he was causing – not least because his campaign of harassment echoed the one that Nancy had earlier conducted against him.

Nancy was the girl he identified with the Devil during his first, prophetic acid trip. She was part of the early Marilyn Manson stageshow, indulging in sex acts while being subjected to increasingly grotesque physical abuse by the singer, duly falling in love with her onstage abuser. (One of Nietzsche's most notorious dictums – 'You are going to women – do not forget the whip!' – echoes sinisterly in the background.)

Even Missi, the girl later identified by Marilyn as the most important person in his

SEXUAL CHEMISTRY

Baphomet - a form of the devil
popularised by the nineteenth-century
French occultist Eliphas Levi.

Perhaps the most familiar occult androgyne – a figure that unites or transcends the two sexes – is the image of Satan as a goat-headed creature with woman's breasts and an erect penis. Commonly referred to as Baphomet, this image of the Devil has both male and female organs to emphasise his status as a lord of carnal lust and earthly pleasure. The original 'god of fuck', if you will.

The androgyne is very important in many occult traditions. Alchemists of the Middle Ages and the Renaissance, who attempted to turn base metals like lead into gold, were also searching for a way to render the human soul into its purest form. The androgyne, or hermaphrodite, was of great significance to the symbolic language of the alchemist, representing transcendence of the limitations that bind a human being to a specific gender.

The name of Marilyn Manson's latest persona, Mercury, refers to the alchemical element that was, according to some secret teachings, purer than gold. The literal essence of transformation and perfection, according to one eighteenth century German text, Mercury is 'beginning, middle and end, it is the copulator, the priest who brings all things together and conjoins them'. 'It represents both the androgyne and the *prima materia*,' explained Marilyn when introducing his new insignia/identity, 'which is then associated with Adam, the first man.'

life, is roped into one of his macabre pranks. They begin going out together at the same time that Florida is being terrorised by a brutal serial killer who targets young girls, dubbed the Gainseville Slasher by the press. (The killer, Danny Rolling, would later write his memoirs – published as *The Making of a Serial Killer* by Feral House, publishers of much of Anton LaVey's work.) More than a little tastelessly, Marilyn saw the activities of the killer as an opportunity for a morbid practical joke – shooting a series of intimate polaroids of his girlfriend Missi, made-up to look as if they were photos of a sexually abused corpse. The gory, sexually explicit shots were discarded in public places, to be chanced upon by any hapless concerned citizen.

Asked if he was popular with girls as a teenager, the Antichrist Superstar responded candidly, 'I liked them but I didn't have much luck with them. I went through a bit of a

DRESSED TO KILL

There is a curious connection between killers and cross-dressing a connection illustrated by three of the murderers incorporated by Marilyn Manson band-members into their stage names.

During his traumatic childhood Charlie Manson was, for a time, looked after by his pious aunt and uncle, who insisted the unfortunate kid attend school in a girl's dress to toughen him up. The story is echoed in the upbringing of Henry Lee Lucas, also in the Southern USA of the 1940s, whose violently abusive mother sent him to school with permed hair and girl's clothing. The Texan misfit grew up to become an alcoholic drifter, falling in with another feral vagrant named Ottis Toole who had also been dressed as a girl during a fearsomely abusive childhood. When the police apprehended Lucas in 1983 on a firearms charge, he surprised his captors with a mind-blowing catalogue of confessions, detailing an orgy of torture, rape and murder that had taken him across America with his partner and lover Toole. However much or however little of his confessions may have been true, Henry Lee Lucas' notoriety inspired erstwhile Marilyn Manson drummer Sara Lee Lucas to adopt half his name.

Perhaps the most bizarre transvestite killer was Ed Gein, who inspired the Manson moniker Gidget Gein. Possibly guilty of only two murders and numerous acts of grave robbery, the sheer grotesquerie of his crimes assured the criminal a place in American folklore and serial murder studies. Brought up by a domineering, religious mother, Ed grew into a socially retarded handyman in the isolated Wisconsin community in which he lived. When his mother died, Gein's eccentricities seemed to multiply, though none of his neighbours guessed just how far.

He was arrested in 1957, when the body of a local woman was found hung in his shed and gutted like a deer. The details of his crimes were largely suppressed as too horrible for public consumption at the time, but were later absorbed into popular legend. Perhaps the most bizarre was Gein's propensity for draping himself in the skin of dead women and cavorting about beneath the moon. This memorable image inspired classic horror movies as diverse in style as *Psycho*, *The Texas Chainsaw Massacre* and *The Silence of the Lambs* all emphasising different aspects of Gein's gruesome obsession with female flesh. In *Silence . . .* , Gein was the prototype for the loathsome Buffalo Bill character, a sexual 'skin transvestite', while *Psycho*'s Norman Bates was a cross-dressing momma's boy who kept Mom's stuffed corpse in the cellar, very different from Leatherface, the brutally subhuman man behind the mask-of-flesh in *Chainsaw . . .* , who lived, Gein-style, in a farmhouse decorated with human body parts.

KISS THIS!

Marilyn Manson's fondness for impromptu exhibitionism means his trousers rarely stay up for an entire performance. Whether he's wiping it on a Bible, the American flag, or simply displaying his butt to the audience, it's fair to say his fans are more familiar with Marilyn's ass than he is. One of the dominant images of the 1990s is of this slender performer mooning at America – from a Freudian viewpoint, feeding the USA's anal fixation.

There is a traditional connection between 'anal' and 'evil': showing somebody your backside has always been an insult, even in ancient times. Anal sex is still illegal in many places and remains a taboo, a dirty, wholly non-procreative sex act – one in the eye for Christianity, which preaches that all sex for pleasure, rather than procreation, is sinful. Back in the tenth century, a heretical Christian sect called the Bogomils, who practised anal sex because they thought procreation itself was sinful, inspired the word 'buggery'. According to medieval tradition, Satan's ass was his best feature – illustrations from this time usually picture him with a face on his behind. Witches were supposed to adore their satanic master by kissing him on the backside, a practice known as the 'osculum infame' ('obscene kiss'), or kiss of shame.

misogynist period, because I was resentful that I didn't have any luck and I had a big heartbreak, but then I turned to writing and started the band, and that became my escape from worrying about girls. When you listen to our early songs, there are a lot of spiteful lyrics about relationships which come from that period.'

Ultimately, accusations of misogyny may be deflected by his adoption of a partly feminine persona. Would a man who hated women adopt some of their characteristics with such enthusiasm? The themes of abuse inherent in Marilyn Manson are about a series of human conflicts, not just the war between the sexes, and recognising that it cuts both ways. 'I've grown up,' the band's leader observes on the topic of abuse and misogyny. 'I don't think I've ever misused anyone because of their looks. People have to choose a role in life. Either they're a user or they're someone who will be used, and those people should just be thankful that they're even useful.' (Echoing LaVey's dictum that it's better to be used than useless.)

Inevitably, however, Marilyn's toying with gender led many to speculate about his sexuality. 'I'm playing with the subject,' he once commented. 'People tend to be so uptight about it. I just wanted to make it less of a taboo. And at the end of the rules, it states that I've broken all of them. A lot of people are afraid to talk about or address homosexuality – and there's always so many rumours directed towards me and my sexuality.'

Public displays like giving a blow-job to a member of Nine Inch Nails on stage did little to discourage these rumours. 'People's fears start to come out when you do something

TRANVESTITES AND TRANSGRESSIVES

By no means do all cross-dressers choose to cross the gender gap to demonstrate their homosexuality. In fact, many transvestites are greatly offended at suggestions that they adopt feminine garb because they're gay. In the entertainment and artistic worlds, the motive is often to deliberately challenge accepted ideas about gender and identity. There's nothing new in using cross-dressing to challenge social taboo. Christmas has its origins in a pagan Ancient Roman winter festival named Saturnalia, which the Christians adapted for their own purposes. Saturnalia, however, was originally a celebration of fun and mischief in the face of the grim winter season, where many taboos and customs were overturned for a day and men dressed as women.

In modern pop-culture, this same flouting of convention is alive and well. The Rolling Stones, archetypal bad boys of 1960s rock'n'roll, outraged the establishment with their outrageous camp which reached a peak with the cover art for the 1966 single 'Have You Seen Your Mother Baby?', featuring the band dressed as rather unprepossessing women. At the same time, pop artist Andy Warhol, who later became an influential figure on the fringes of the glam-rock scene, was welcoming transvestites into his New York 'Factory' to appear in art-house movies like *Trash*. In the following decade, cult trash director John Waters would try to make the glamorously grotesque transvestite Divine into a star in such cinematic gross-outs as *Pink Flamingos* and *Desperate Living* (both later plundered for samples by Marilyn Manson.)

The most outrageous cross-dresser to emerge from Warhol's Factory was Wayne County (later Jayne County). County was a performer in his (her) own right, best remembered for the songs 'Are You Man Enough To Be a Woman?' and '(If You Don't Wanna Fuck Me, Baby) Fuck Off'. It was County's live show that was most memorable, however. According to a 1971 review in *Crawdaddy* magazine, it took New York's embryonic androgynous gender-bending scene 'to its logical conclusion . . . County's act is carried on in total drag; he wears a plastic cunt with straw hair, sucks off a large dildo, shoots "come" at the audience with a plastic squirt gun, and for an encore eats dogfood out of a toilet bowl . . . while these groups and their fans on this burgeoning scene profess to be parodying or "camping on" various sexual styles (bisexuality, transvestism, sadomasochism), it is difficult to say where affectation ends and reality begins.'

However, few cross-dressing phenomena have achieved the same cult kudos as Tim Curry playing the 'sweet transvestite from Transexual Transylvania', Dr Frank N. Furter, the anti-hero of the hit musical/cult movie *The Rocky Horror Show*. Marilyn has described the lingerie-clad Curry as 'a hot number. I would have liked him to shave his armpits though. I'm not big on them. Is have mine.

I can't even look at myself with armpit hair. Disgusting!' Ostensibly a camp send-up of cheap horror and science fiction movies, *The Rocky Horror Show* carries a mischievous subtext that makes outrageous sexual perversity look like fun, while conformity is overtly dull and depressing. The cinematic version, *The Rocky Horror Picture Show*, has long been a cult hit, with countless fans, male and female, attending performances in fishnet-stocking drag to get into the spirit of things. Its blend of campy gothic horror with sexual fetishism also made it a big favourite among the gothic subculture.

Tim Curry camps it up as Dr Frank N. Furter in The Rocky Horror Picture Show.

like that,' Manson observed. 'A lot of macho guys started calling me "faggot", wanted to start a fight with me. Why would they want to fight me because I did that? Obviously it scared them. I'm confident enough with my sexuality where I can do something like that. Anyone who knows me, knows I like girls.' So why invite the rumours?

The answer only partly lies in the response his behaviour inspires. When asked whether invoking homosexuality as a taboo didn't reinforce the prejudice that it was 'evil' or 'wrong', Marilyn responded, 'I perceive decadence and "evil", quote/unquote, as a good thing. So when I perpetuate it and slap it in the face of conservative people, it's like these things are the things that I like, and these are the things that I find entertaining and fulfilling. And I know it makes you mad, and I want you to be mad, because I enjoy it. And I want them to be pissed off that I enjoy it. I don't just use it as a button to push. Because, you see, it's not just "What can I do next to make them mad?" It's not something that I wouldn't do anyway at home just for my own enjoyment, because I've done plenty of things that people haven't heard about, just for kicks, that I wasn't doing, you know, to piss someone off.'

But there's more to his interest in gender taboos than a desire to shock. Freudian analysis might locate its origins way back in the childhood of Brian Warner. The story that opens his autobiography – of his illicit visits to the cellar where his grandfather indulges his unusual sexual habits – clearly had a great impact. The old man used a dildo and, as the boy later discovered, wore women's underwear under his work clothes, coming to light when Grandfather Jack was involved in an accident while working as a trucker and had to be taken to hospital.

When he was eight or nine years old, Marilyn recalls in his autobiography, an older neighbourhood boy named Mark who coerced him into playing 'prison' – a dubious-sounding game whereby Brian would squeeze into a dumbwaiter, naked because the imaginary guards would not allow the inmates even the most basic of comforts. Once crammed into their claustrophobic 'cell', Marilyn claims his cellmate Mark would caress him and try to play with young Brian's dick.

However traumatic these early experiences may have been, the origins of Marilyn Manson can once more be traced to the Christian Heritage School, where the young misfit used his teachers' blacklist of forbidden records as a source of recommendations. He recalls that his Christian tutors reserved special condemnation for Queen, notably because they regarded the band's song 'We Are the Champions' as a gay anthem, and because, they maintained, it contained the words 'My Sweet Satan' if played backwards. Other bands with perceived or authentic homosexual connections were also forbidden to the pupils, with vocalists like David Bowie and Adam Ant portrayed as illustrating the axis between homosexuality and evil.

Contrary to what modern liberal Christians would have you believe, God hates homosexuals and cross-dressers – at least, that's what it says in The Bible. The Book of Leviticus states that, 'If a man also lie with mankind, as he lieth with a woman, both of them have committed an abomination: they shall surely be put to death; their blood shall be upon them.' The Book of Deuteronomy commands, 'The woman shall not wear that which pertaineth unto a man, neither shall a man put on a woman's garment: for all that do so are abominations unto the Lord thy God.'

According to rock journalist Albert Goldman, the 1970s saw a revival of the Decadent movement. 'By whatever mysterious underground channels the decadent sensibility has been conveyed from nineteenth century Paris and London to twentieth century New York,' he wrote in 1974. 'The fact is that we are living unconsciously, inadvertently, rather casually, the dread, degenerate, opium-dream existence fantasised by radical writers a hundred years ago. Everybody's walking around in crushed velvet and Parisian brothel boots. People's faces are painted up like Toulouse-Lautrec *demi-mondaines*. They're as languorous as dandies, as jaded as aesthetes, as narcoleptic as absinthe drinkers.'

While Goldman was wrong inasmuch as the more radical Decadents of the nineteenth century did more than just fantasise their lifestyles, there were definitely parallels with the 1970s. This particular scene was known, in its English birthplace, as 'glam'. Its chief pioneer was Marc Bolan, a singer with effeminately elfin good looks whose androgynous style (including feather boas and glitter jackets) helped propel him to stardom. According to his producer, Tony Visconti, 'There was a place in the World's End that sold clothes that were considered kind of kitsch. That famous chartreuse satin jacket with the music notes embroidered on it – this was pure kitsch, and musicians weren't really dressing like that yet. Marc took it very seriously and started walking around like that. I don't remember anyone before him wearing those vivid colours.'

Many trace the birth of the movement to a 1971 performance by Bolan's band, T. Rex, on the UK TV show *Top of the Pops*. He performed with heavy eye make-up and glitter sprinkled on his perfect cheekbones. Bolan's manager David Enthovan recalls, 'As soon as he got on TV, basically it all took off. Marc definitely started it. He was the first to put glitter on his face, and I think it had a lot to do with his wife. June had the vision about how to present this little pixie. It was definitely a team.' Bolan was soon joined by another Englishman – his friend and rival David Bowie, whose wife and early inspiration, Angie, had a flair for androgynous chic. While Bolan was the consummate pop star, sparkling and pretty but devoid of substance, Bowie's survival instinct inspired him to constantly change, going through a bewildering array of artistic incarnations.

In the early 1970s Bowie decamped to the USA, encountering New York's caustic but vibrant young art and music scene – as well as the androgynes of Andy Warhol's Factory. In America at this point, 'glitter rock' was the common description for the new, flamboyantly androgynous rock'n'roll. As Bebe Buell, a veteran of the New York scene, recalls, the US scene developed along more aggressive lines, into an underground that gave birth to the nascent US punk scene rather than a mainstream commercial craze. 'It was a marriage of punk and glitter, whereas in Britain it was either punk or glitter. You see, the street life of Manhattan was the wild side. The only thing you could compare

David Bowie, as an artist, has both influenced and been a point of comparison for Marilyn Manson. Born David Jones in London, 1947, his determination to achieve pop stardom took him through various early incarnations as a hippie, mod and cabaret singer, all well-promoted commercial failures. It wasn't until he hitched himself to the embryonic glam scene that this striking, androgynous performer truly began his climb to stardom.

Prior to his commercial breakthrough, the 1970 album *The Man Who Sold the World*, a darkly brooding record with heavy metal flourishes, boasted the singer lounging on the cover in a dress. It set the tone for much of the ensuing decade with its decadent themes of sexual deviance, decay and insanity, influenced by the darkest elements of Aleister Crowley and Friedrich Nietzsche (figures who would loom large in the world of Marilyn Manson two decades later).

These same occultic and philosophical influences bled into the more melodic, sugar-coated 1971 follow-up *Hunky Dory*, but it failed to achieve the commercial success his label anticipated. Around the time of the album's release, however, Bowie's off-the-cuff admission of bisexuality made him a hot item with the press. *The Rise and Fall of Ziggy Stardust and the Spiders from Mars* was his big breakthrough, an album which successfully married his artistic pretensions, unique vision and talent for theatrical display with infectiously catchy songs. Apocalyptic, futuristic, decadent, the singer took on the persona of the title character, a rock star whose internal destruction mirrored the collapse of the world around him, predating Marilyn Manson's take on the same themes by a quarter-of-a-century. The apocalyptic tenor of *Ziggy Stardust* cut close to the bone for Bowie, who began suffering under the increasing pressures of stardom and rock excess during the recording of his next outing, *Aladdin Sane* (a lad insane), which haunts the same fractured territory.

The 1974 recording *Diamond Dogs* featured a three-song cycle loosely based on George Orwell's novel *1984* – a depiction of life in a grim totalitarian state in the near future – alongside material inspired by cult science fiction author Harlan Ellison and drug-culture icon William Burroughs. The prolific vocalist continued to produce albums that showcased his adaptability, from 'plastic rhythm and blues' (*Young Americans*, 1975) to futuristically-tinged soul ballads (*Station to Station*, 1976) and austere semi-instrumental works (*Low*, 1977). Aware of rock's ephemeral obsession with youth, Bowie expanded into other media in the 1980s, refusing to rest on his laurels as a pop icon. He pursued an acting career (most notably in *Merry Christmas, Mr Lawrence* and *The Hunger*, both 1983), recorded movie soundtracks, indulged in a number of improbable duets (his Bing Crosby collaboration raising a few eyebrows) and recorded some upbeat material that finally divorced him from his decadent golden years.

Nevertheless, Bowie's importance as a pioneer in the musical worlds of danceable despair and futuristic frustration was acknowledged in 1995 when Trent Reznor accompanied him on tour, yielding the headline spot to Bowie when Nine Inch Nails were transparently the bigger draw. The *New York Times* observed that, 'While Bowie and Reznor are kindred performers in some ways, they are polar opposites in others. Reznor is an explosive introvert, ranting and agonising over his private torments while Nine Inch Nails hammers blunt, primal riffs. It's clear what's on his mind. Bowie, by contrast, is a detached observer, parcelling out disconnected hints and images, moving in and out of the stories he suggests. His songs are more abstract, even at their most impassioned.'

On *Mechanical Animals*, Marilyn Manson made no attempt to hide the heavy influence of Bowie in his 1970s heyday. Interestingly, the Bowie project most effectively evoked is not a recording but his haunting 1976 feature-film debut, *The Man Who Fell To Earth*. Bowie starred as an alien who comes to earth, hoping to transport water back to his dying desert home planet. The science fiction story is only a metaphor, however, Bowie's alien persona expressing earthly symptoms of alienation – alienation that the singer himself felt as a result of his celebrity status, with all the fragmentation and chemical over-indulgence that accompanied it. The parallels with *Mechanical Animals* are striking: particularly the vision of Bowie as the de-sexed alien in the film, and Marilyn Manson as the androgynous extraterrestrial on the album's cover.

David Bowie in glam rock mode.

it to was pre-war Berlin.'

While touring to promote the seminal glam album *The Rise and Fall of Ziggy Stardust and the Spiders from Mars*, the highly-strung Bowie began to go through another transformation. According to Barney Hoskyns in his book *Glam!*, Bowie's mind was 'teeming with cartoon visions of catastrophe. The songs turned America – the America of 'Panic in Detroit' and 'Drive-in Saturday' [both from the follow-up album to *Ziggy*, *Aladdin Sane*] – into a surreal, polysexual playground, a nation of neon and Quaaludes, a place at once depraved and coldly alienating . . . It suggested a mind teetering on the edge of psychosis, writing under pressure, writhing beneath the spotlight of media attention.' (The parallels here with Marilyn Manson's *Mechanical Animals* are unmistakable.) In May of 1973, however, Bowie, turned his back on the glam scene he helped create, declaring to the British music paper *Melody Maker*, 'This whole decadence thing is a bloody joke. I'm very normal.'

Even though its innovators were moving on, numerous bands continued to carry glam rock's lurid torch through the 1970s. One reason was that, contrary to the initial fears of many wanna-be rock stars, androgyny did not discourage groupies – in fact, quite the reverse. In contrast to the world of nineteenth-century decadence, when androgynes were usually misogynists, the 1970s saw women becoming increasingly comfortable with androgynous or gay men. Brian Eno, electronic prankster with influential early glam band Roxy Music, was known for his outrageously effeminate dress sense.

'Women always seemed to get on with gays,' Eno later reflected, 'and I think it's slightly like that. It's a feeling that there is someone who is other but who is not threatening, who has surrendered their authority and their ability to command by strength. If you're gay or you're androgynous, you're not playing that usual male role of "I'm the tough one here." She knows that this guy isn't playing the male . . . There was a whole kind of negative movement at the same time saying either men were terrible or women were pathetic, and I thought, "Why not just be neither of them? Why not side-step the whole argument by becoming something else, something in between?" I think that's a strong position. And of course it's a position that a lot of people have generally adopted – the New Man is a slightly feminized man, basically.'

Glam lost its outrageous edge as it became acceptable. In the US, KISS borrowed some of the look but adapted it to heavy metal, turning theatrical androgyny into the aggressive, air-headed machismo of 1980s glam-metal bands who incongruously blended hair-spray with testosterone. In the UK, glam introduced androgyny into mainstream pop, opening the door for flamboyantly camp singers like Freddie Mercury of Queen to play to huge, largely homophobic audiences seemingly unaware of the band name's gay subtext. (Something of a barometer for public attitudes to homosexuality, Queen began their career as a glam band, while Mercury, the only bisexual member, only made his sexual preferences public when the band hit the big time.) By the 1980s, chart success was enjoyed by the subversively inoffensive Culture Club, with their cross-dressing singer

Boy George. Discussing glam's heritage, Barney Hoskyns observes, 'Boy George's secret lay in taking the androgyny of glam a stage further, turning himself into a kind of cuddly eunuch. More influential was the female androgyny of the Eurythmics' Annie Lennox, which did for white pop what Grace Jones had done for black disco: more audacious was the pervy "deviance" of Soft Cell's Marc Almond.'

Marilyn Manson, who describes Queen's 1977 album *News of the World* as one of his favourite records, would later guardedly confess to meeting Boy George. Underlining the inane innocuousness of the prancing prima donna, he explained, 'My mom loves Boy George. My mom writes him love letters. He gave my mom his address and she won't stop obsessing about him. She doesn't think he's gay. She thinks she's got a shot at it.'

While trite little pop queen Boy George had little impact on the cultural landscape, Marilyn Manson would create shockwaves felt far beyond the entertainment industry. After their cover of androgyne pop diva Annie Lennox's 'Sweet Dreams' introduced the band to a broader public, and the huge success of *Antichrist Superstar*, the band looked back to their 1970s childhoods for inspiration. The resultant third album, *Mechanical Animals*, dispensed with the harsh, caustic sound of their earlier material in favour of a more accessible, yet deliberately cold and hollow approach. 'This sound reflects the feeling in the record – more dynamic and more melodic – to evoke what I'm speaking of. And the music that did that for me as a kid was Queen, David Bowie, Prince, Kiss . . . T. Rex,' he enthused.

It wasn't just the glam sound of the 1970s and early 1980s that Marilyn wanted to evoke, but its spirit. Glam had been a reaction to the drab worthiness of the music scene at the time. Rock music was dominated by predictable country-rock outfits dressed in denim, and pretentious post-hippie performers with earnest lyrics and acoustic guitars. Glam brought bombastic fun back into rock'n'roll, re-energising it with a splash of colour and glorious irresponsibility. In the 1990s, the Reverend Manson evangelised the same kind of tackiness that rocked the music business two decades back. 'Look at it this way,' he explained, 'grunge killed stardom, all the musicians wanted to be ordinary people, just like their fans. We are the complete opposite; we wanted to bring the glamour and personality back, the showmanship. Grunge never interested me. I wanted theatricality, a big statement and that required an image that had to be extreme . . .'

Of course, Marilyn Manson brought their own distinctive approach to glam rock, with some elements on *Mechanical Animals* that were bleaker than Bowie at his most apocalyptic. Omega, Marilyn Manson's answer to Ziggy Stardust, is as unsettling as he is seductive. 'I was imagining Omega to be the most exaggerated extension of what the Antichrist Superstar was,' he explained, 'everything that glam rock has ever been and then some. To me glam rock has always meant a very sarcastic and over-the-top flamboyant image that was hiding something that was darker and more depressing underneath. That was always the irony of glam rock to me.'

Chapter Six

PRINCIPLES OF PLEASURE AND PAIN

'The world doesn't revolve around the sun,' Marilyn Manson once declared, 'it revolves around a giant cock. That is what the world is about; it's about sex. Anybody who doesn't want to realise that is fooling themselves . . . People are bored because they've done everything they can do, so now the fear of death is the only thing that gets them excited. That's why people have made me into some kind of sex symbol. I'm death on wheels, the way I look.'

Man, as a species, has always had sex on the brain, though the forms it takes have varied over the years. The 1990s have been characterised by a rise in the public profile of fetishism, particularly sadomasochism, springing from its grassroots in the counterculture.

It seems we were all ready for a sex symbol who was 'death on wheels' – Marilyn took to the role as if born to it, staking out the unsettling territory between pain and pleasure. The Manson stageshow is a perverse celebration of lust and fury. Even the audience, clad in leather, PVC and rubber, wear their marks of self-mutilation like battle scars. Few images from *The Long Hard Road Out of Hell* are as simultaneously grotesque and affecting as the photo of the 'slash girls' with 'Marilyn' and 'Manson' carved into their chests.

When Marilyn spoke of 'a giant cock' he was referring to the sexual theories of Sigmund Freud, but he might as well have been quoting the occult doctrine of Aleister Crowley. In his book *The Magical World of Aleister Crowley*, Francis King describes the Great Beast's strange cosmology: 'For Crowley . . . the sun was the supreme deity. On earth however he is represented by the phallus, the male sexual organ, which is "the vice-regent of the sun", "the sole giver of life". All the universal gods – that is deities such as the gods and goddesses of the moon, of fire, of mountains and of trees – are, it is asserted, but personifications of the penis. Thus the fire-deity is an image of the sun "and a fable of the phallus"; the tree is "but the flowering of the Phallus", while the moon-deity is an image of the vagina . . .'

Crowley believed in the occult doctrine that preaches how the cosmos is reflected in the human body, and vice versa. As he also believed that the most profound human experience was sexual orgasm, he reasoned that sex was the central power of the cosmos. This was a central credo of 'Crowleyanity' – in the Great Beast's creed, most religious rituals and magical workings were accompanied – as with oriental philosophies like Tantrism, which Crowley had studied – by sexual acts.

Freud shared Crowley's conviction that sex was the key to understanding our place in the universe, though he dismissed religion as a symptom of widespread neuroses. Indeed, his later years were occupied by the search for an impulse strong enough to deny the sexual urge, therefore explaining why human behaviour wasn't solely motivated by sex. Freud came up with an interesting solution: the sexual urge of Eros (Ancient Greek god of lust) was in direct conflict with the death urge of Thanatos (Ancient Greek god of death). Our instinct to reproduce ourselves was balanced by our instinct to die. According to Freud, the interplay between these conflicting instincts, and their development during childhood, determined our adult hang-ups and perversions.

It would be intriguing to know what Freud would have made of Aleister Crowley. As a child, Crowley was heavily disciplined by his strict Christian parents and teachers. As an adult, he responded by turning his sexual urges into the basis of an anti-Christian religion with himself as its prophet. Sex and death figure heavily in Crowleyanity, with its rites of blood and eroticism, as do masters and slaves – Crowley's cosmology having much in common with Nietzsche's vision of a master-morality and slave-morality, transcending ordinary ideas of good and evil. Marilyn Manson would later echo this harsh worldview by observing, 'When you break it down, in life some people like to be abused, and some people like to abuse other people. In reality that's not such a bad thing, you just have to pick your role in life. Sometimes I'm both.'

Sexual fetishism was evident in many of the rites and ceremonies undertaken by the Great Beast. In 1909, Crowley subjected his new apprentice, Victor Neuburg, to a 'magical retirement' – a crash course in the occult that reads very much like a heavily sadomasochistic homosexual fling. As Francis King observes, 'it is clear that both men had strongly sado-masochistic elements in their make-up – even in the brutal discipline inflicted by Zen Buddhist masters on their pupils there is nothing to compare with the incidents when Crowley beat his pupil with gorse and nettles'. In early 1914, the Great Beast engaged with Neuberg in the 'Paris workings', magical rites with the aim of invoking the gods Jupiter and Mercury who, the pair hoped, would provide them with much-needed funds.

These homosexual rites reached an even greater sadomasochistic intensity when Crowley not only beat his disciple, but also bound him with chains and carved a cross over his heart. (Interestingly, however, in acts of sodomy Crowley almost always took the passive role.) One of the climaxes of these rites was a vision of a past life in Ancient Crete – when Crowley was a dancing girl and Neuberg a novice priest, both enslaved as punishment for falling in love with each other. In Crowley's world of sacred sadomasochism and hallowed whores, we witness a man trying to exorcise his Christian childhood of sexual repression and harsh corporal punishment.

Anton LaVey often described his Church of Satan as an institution designed to occupy 'the grey area between psychiatry and religion', a doctrine perhaps best illustrated in its attitude toward sex. Psychiatry sought to 'cure' sexual peculiarities or perversions, while religion sought either to suppress (as with Christianity) or disguise (as with Crowleyanity) the carnal urge. The Church of Satan, on the other hand, celebrated fetishes and fantasies as badges of individuality. According to LaVeyan Satanism, individualism is the central factor: the person who indulges in promiscuity in order to take part in the sexual revolution is no more 'free' than the person who avoids 'disreputable' sexual behaviour. Satanic sex is not, as some imagine, an orgy of non-stop promiscuity so much as an orgy of whatever truly turns you on – even if that is total abstinence.

In the chapter on 'Satanic Sex' in *The Satanic Bible*, LaVey wrote, 'Satanism condones any type of sexual activity which properly satisfies your individual desires – be it heterosexual, homosexual, bisexual, or even asexual, if you choose. Satanism also sanctions any fetish or deviation which will enhance your sex-life, so long as it involves no one who does not wish to be involved.

'The prevalence of deviant and/or fetishistic behaviour in our society would stagger the imagination of the sexually naïve. There are more sexual variants than the enlightened individual can perceive: transvestism, sadism, masochism, urolagnia, exhibitionism – to name only a few of the more predominant. Everyone has some form of fetish, but because they are unaware of the preponderance of fetishistic activity in our society, they feel they are depraved if they submit to their "unnatural" yearnings.'

While fetishism is a broad term, covering a wide range of different sexual proclivities and erotic obsessions, somehow sadomasochism and dominance/submission – the erotic exchange of power and pain between partners – seem to be the flagship of the deviant fleet. Perhaps this is because of the flamboyant paraphernalia of whips, chains and leather, or its uniting of the apparent opposites of pleasure and pain. Or perhaps, as Freud suggested, pain and pleasure are not incompatible opposites but different sides of the same coin, with sadomasochism bringing us uncomfortably close to that truth.

Freud was not alone in reaching this uncomfortable conclusion. In his book *Sexual Anomalies and Perversions*, Magnus Hirschfeld recalled a particularly haunting experience that underlined the relationship, at least for some, between Eros and Thanatos. Hirschfeld was in Berlin in 1919 (at the dawn of the German decadent era), when, after a political uprising was bloodily suppressed, he was asked to accompany 'a woman to the mortuary where, among hundreds of bodies, some of which were shockingly mutilated or had their throats slit, we discovered her son . . . In the identification hall an endless stream of people, mainly women, were filing past the unidentified bodies and an attendant who knew me called my attention to some girls who had for several days continually rejoined

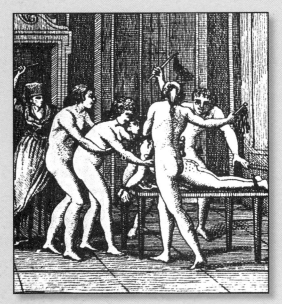

A late-eighteenth-century engraving depicting one of the many orgies in the Marquis de Sade's epics of sadism and sex.

The term 'sadism' is derived from an eighteenth-century French nobleman named Donatien Alphonse de Sade. It's surprising, perhaps, that the Marquis de Sade, whose name has become synonymous with the ultimate cruelty, should have many admirers – but, since his death in 1814, his work has been enthusiastically applauded by Decadent writers, surrealist artists, and even some feminists. A nobly born, squat-figured cavalry officer, de Sade was distinguished by a lively mind and an even livelier sex drive. His kinky tastes ran to whipping and being whipped, and erotic games with hot wax, as well as both heterosexual and homosexual sex (which still carried the penalty of death under French law at this time). As an ardent atheist – some say Satanist – the Marquis also introduced blasphemy into some of his orgies, giving them the flavour of improvised Black Masses.

Because of his high birth, if de Sade had confined his adventures to lowly prostitutes and maintained a level of discretion, he could probably have pursued his unorthodox love life without legal interference. But, in 1763, he married into a respectable middle-class family. De Sade hoped to share their wealth in exchange for the prestige of his aristocratic name, but his scandalous reputation made him a public embarrassment to his new in-laws. In exasperation, de Sade's mother-in-law arranged to have her unrepentantly deviant relative imprisoned in 1777, and he was to spend most of the rest of his life in gaols and lunatic asylums. It was here that de Sade was to write the stories that made him notorious. Meticulously, secretively, by candlelight, the Marquis de Sade wrote pornographic epics detailing acts of sexual cruelty and perversity that easily eclipsed anything he ever attempted in real life.

Indeed, many of his modern champions claim that, while he may have had unusual sexual tastes, de Sade was not by nature a cruel man.

The prostitutes he hired consented to be whipped, and when fate, in the shape of the French Revolution, put the life of his mother-in-law into his hands, 'Citizen Sade' spared the woman who had been responsible for so much of his own misery. But de Sade placed no fetters on his imagination, allowing it to roam freely through his darkest sadomasochistic fantasies. However, it is the philosophy woven into his pornographic stories that has most intrigued his posthumous admirers.

The Marquis de Sade's religious philosophy displays an atheistic attitude so militant it borders upon Satanism. His observation that the universe is actively cruel and unjust is best expressed in the twin novels *Justine* and *Juliette*, about two sisters – one of whom is virtuous and suffers terribly for it, the other who is wicked and prospers because of it. The books are subtitled *The Misfortunes of Virtue* and *The Prosperity of Vice*: the same idea reflected in Anton LaVey's maxim, 'No good deed goes unpunished.'

De Sade's ideas on law and society reflect a similar attitude. He reasoned that we should follow our natural inclinations rather than the dictates of an imaginary god, and if we felt natural urges towards sex or violence then it was more sinful to suppress such urges than to express them. Whether he every truly believed this, or whether it was just a symptom of his deep frustration at being imprisoned for so long, is difficult to say. But the Marquis de Sade's perverse philosophy of total freedom has excited, outraged and inspired people long after his small-minded oppressors have been all but forgotten. Like every challenging philosophy, this has its distinctly dark side: while several modern commentators see de Sade as a radical advocate of personal liberty, a few criminals have used his writings as philosophical justification for their crimes. The most obvious example is the British serial killer Ian Brady, a devotee of the notorious Marquis, who, with his partner Myra Hindley, committed a murderous series of sexual atrocities against children in the 1960s.

the queue, evidently because they could not tear themselves away from the sight of the male bodies which lay, entirely stripped, before them . . . The expression on their faces was similar to that which I had seen when the women of Madrid and Seville watch the bull-fighters in the ring.'

Hirschfeld later notes that the Marquis de Sade had witnessed women surreptitiously masturbating at public executions, which were noted as good pick-up locations by young men. Classical literature also records that the Roman empresses Messalina and Theodora masturbated while watching gladiatorial combat.

While Freud used sex to map out the human mind, and Crowley employed it to chart the mystical world, LaVey regarded sex as an allegorical guide to human society. In his biography, *The Secret Life of a Satanist*, the chapter dedicated to 'Masochistic America' suggests that the Black Pope's experiments in sadomasochistic ritual and psychodrama in the 1960s could profitably be applied wholesale to the present-day USA.

LaVey diagnoses the major problem of Western society as an epidemic of unrecognised masochism. Overt masochism is harmless, admirable even, as an honest expression of an individual's identity. But the repressed masochism brought about by the confused messages broadcast from TV set or church pulpit – which simultaneously tell the masses they're all worthy individuals while reminding them of their inadequacies – just create self-important zombies with a subconscious desire to be punished. And all too often, such covert masochism manifests itself as attempts to provoke better-developed or more powerful individuals into punishing them. By this typically perverse line of argument, LaVey presents the thugs and hooligans used to justify repressive laws of Church and State as malfunctioning masochists created by those very same institutions. 'Most people don't want to pick a leader,' says LaVey, 'they want to pick an executioner. So when they "elect a leader" they're really saying "I want you to pull the switch, not the other one."'

In 1998, the year following his death, a requiem was held for Anton LaVey at London's Torture Garden in recognition of his role in promoting an understanding of fetishism. The club's name is derived from a 1899 book by Octave Mirbeau. One of the most macabre Decadent novels, *The Torture Garden* describes an elegantly depraved Englishwoman introducing a cynical Frenchman to the immoral delights of a Chinese garden where torture is practised as an art form. Brutal sadism and unspeakable beauty become inextricably intertwined like two poisonous vines, in this novel which Oscar Wilde referred to as 'a green adder of a book'.

The Torture Garden is just one of dozens of popular fetish clubs operating in most Western cities today, high-profile concerns open to anyone willing to pay the entrance fee and wear the appropriate fetishistic costume. Such clubs would have been unthinkable thirty years ago, at the time of the foundation of the Church of Satan. By 1990 the unimaginable had started to happen, and S/M nightclubs – once a secretive domain confined to the red light districts of Europe's most liberal cities – started to surface above ground. So where did these popular fetishist night-spots emerge from, and why do so many fashionable young people attend?

It isn't that such clubs didn't use to exist – but they were private, discreet affairs, part of an erotic underworld where wealthy deviants rubbed shoulders with petty criminals, prostitutes and maverick artists. It was an underworld that the Decadents of the 1890s had been very familiar with. Just as in the 1990s, when Marilyn Manson, the band, summoned up the most exotically grotesque 'sex workers' they could find to liven up their recording sessions, so poets like Baudelaire and the flagellant masochist Algernon Swinburne were familiar faces in the flesh pots of the 1890s. In the erotic underworld of the bath-house and brothel, the contrast between the beauty of carnal love and the sordid nature of forbidden vice proved irresistible.

Oscar Wilde described his own predilection for hunting down young rent boys in London's dingy backstreets in typically decadent prose: 'It was like feasting with panthers. The danger was half the excitement. I used to feel as the snake-charmer must feel when he lures the cobra to stir from the painted cloth or reed-basket that holds it, and makes it spread its hood at his bidding, to sway to and fro in the air as a plant sways restlessly in a stream. They were to me the brightest of gilded snakes. Their poison was part of their perfection.'

Gen, lead-singer with radical fetish rockers The Genitorturers, born from the same Florida underground that spawned Marilyn Manson.

A century later, when Marilyn Manson frequented a New York S/M-themed restaurant named La Nouvelle Justine (after the De Sade novel *Justine*), there may have been less of a sense of 'feasting with panthers'. All the same, greater and greater extremes have been introduced into the public arena in order to recapture the thrill. At London's Torture Garden, members pin their lips together with needles, hang from the ceiling with catheters applied to their genitals and grind at their own metal-clad crotches with industrial power tools. In fact, these exotic scenes can be perused in two fully-illustrated coffee-table books on the Torture Garden, available from most good bookshops.

Interested spectators can also subscribe to the glossy, prestigious fetish publication *Skin Two*, or watch an art-house movie extolling the virtues of the fetish scene, like *Preaching to the Perverted*.

In short, fetishism – if not wholly respectable – is not the illicit activity it was one hundred, thirty or even ten years ago. Tattoos, nipple rings and other body-modifications, once the self-inflicted mark of the outsider and outlaw, are now mere fashion statements. Even the most outrageous scenes – like the Torture Garden – are struggling to retain their cutting edge against a tide of fashionable, mainstream acceptance. In several ways this is a good thing – Oscar Wilde was ultimately gaoled for 'feasting with panthers', and renounced his decadent past. On the other hand, it renders the whole business rather toothless. Robbed of its element of danger and taboo, the sexual underworld is in danger of becoming a sterile place where fake fetishism is merchandised for another generation of conformist consumers. So how did we get to this position, and will such tolerance become ultimately tedious?

In the 1980s, the increasing danger posed by AIDS began to make the idea of unorthodox sexual practices like fetishism more attractive. Added to all this, fetishism was becoming 'sexier' as it became trendier. During the first half of this century, it had a real image problem: it was the province of pin-striped perverts, a vice for fat, balding bank managers and bored, middle-aged suburban couples. To outsiders it appeared simultaneously sleazy and sad. The women seen wielding the whips in *Skin Two*, however, are sexy young dominatrices, while the scene now boasts a daring and vitality many hip celebrities are happy to be associated with. It's become slick and sexy, but, inevitably, has started to lose its dangerous edge in the process.

This transformation owes a lot to both rock'n'roll and youth counterculture. In the same way that entertainers gradually made homosexuality acceptable in the late twentieth century, and glam culture helped make camp chic, youth culture has made studs and leather cool. Tattoos were previously rites of passage in macho blue-collar worlds like prisons and army barracks – through the biker subculture they became marks of defiance for rebellious youth. (Rockers were more likely than hippies to see the inside of a prison cell, and the biker cult was largely born of ex-servicemen – the Hell's Angels were originally a US Air Force squadron.) Black leather, for so long the fabric of choice in the fetish community, became the uniform for a generation of teenage rebels. Punk, with its hunger for shock, brought crude piercing and outrageous bondage gear out of the closet and onto the high street.

But all of this was window-dressing, fetish icons taken out of context for effect. Authentic fetishism didn't become hip until the 1990s, after the 1989 publication of the Re/Search book *Modern Primitives*. Still a startling publication today, *Modern Primitives* documents in frank interviews and eye-wateringly graphic photographs the excesses explored by the most daring pioneers of the sexual underworld.

The book soon became a well-thumbed artefact in both penthouse and squat, one of the most shocking items in the counterculture library of the 1990s. Prophetically, *Modern Primitives* recounts a recorded discussion between Anton LaVey, Blanche Barton, Temple ov Psychic Youth founder Genesis P-Orridge and editor V. Vale. P-Orridge wonders if 'this *Modern Primitives* book is just going to encourage people to emulate and mimic . . . like people becoming junkies to emulate William Burroughs, or people going to prison to emulate Jean Genet?'

The editor responds that it's okay if it does, because he sees the movement as 'a statement against Christianity' – appropriately enough, as the idea of sadomasochism and body-modification as a gateway to spirituality had already become a central doctrine of the modern primitive movement. The book opens with a long interview with Fakir Musafar: an American advertising executive whose spare time is occupied by extreme sadomasochistic rituals, deliberately modelled on the ceremonial practices of primitive tribes who use pain to achieve altered states of consciousness. The idea of a return to exotic, pre-Christian practices that horrify straight society was appealing to the readers of *Modern Primitives*. Thus, the 1990s counterculture would adopt S/M and scarification as a self-conscious spiritual or religious statement.

The idea of masochism as a spiritual practice is nothing new. Crowley had conceived of a faith with sadomasochistic sex as a sacrament, and, whatever V. Vale may believe about the anti-Christian nature of S/M, many have identified deep, unconscious sadomasochistic elements in Roman Catholic iconography. In fact, its imagery of ecstatic martyred saints has been interpreted by some as little more than holy porn – such as the image of Saint Sebastian, whose arrow-studded body has become a homo-erotic icon.

As identified by LaVey, the whole ethos of the Christian faith may be seen as masochistic when symbolised by the cross – the very object that its messiah was tortured to death upon. Aldous Huxley's 1956 book *Heaven and Hell* speculates on the relationship between self-induced suffering and religious ecstasy, as in the case of the Christian 'Desert Fathers' – the prototype for the medieval monastic orders, who developed much of the Church's early dogma while living uncomfortable, deprived lives of self-enforced exile in a hostile wasteland. Terence Sellers, in her classic manual of sadomasochistic etiquette, *The Correct Sadist*, observes that 'sadomasochism enjoys all the forms of religious piety – kneeling, praying, worshipping, sacrifice, invoking and punishing'.

While the primitivism of the modern primitive movement concerned itself with the religious aspects of sadomasochism, its modern side assimilated new medical theories on the connections between pleasure and pain. The term 'masochism', like its counterpart 'sadism', was derived from a specific historical figure. Leopold von Sacher-Masoch, an Austrian, wrote his 1869 novel *Venus in Furs* to indulge his obsession with being punished, preferably whipped, by a dominant woman – particularly if she was dressed in furs. The purely fetishistic desires of Sacher-Masoch are emphasised by the fact that there is no conventional sex at all in his book, and the main characters remain clothed throughout.

BLOOD AND SPIRIT

One of the first truly unsettling photographs in *Modern Primitives* shows Fakir Musafar hanging from a tree by two hooks through his nipples, performing the Native American O-Kee-Pa ceremony. Better known as the Sun Dance, this extremely painful ritual was voluntarily undertaken by Sioux Indians who wished to receive divine visions, until the US government banned it in 1904. In the accompanying interview, Musafar quotes from an 1867 description of the original ritual: 'An inch or more of flesh on each shoulder, or each breast, was taken up between the thumb and finger of the man who held the knife; and the knife, which had been hacked and notched to make it produce as much pain as possible, was forced through the flesh below the fingers, and was followed by a skewer which the other attendant forced through the wounds . . . There were then two cords lowered from the top of the lodge, which were fastened to these skewers, and they immediately began to haul him up . . . The fortitude with which every one of them bore this part of the torture surpassed credulity.'

Modern Primitives also contains an essay by Wes Christensen on the self-mutilation rites of Central American tribes like the Maya and Aztecs: 'Unlike the regular penance of routine bloodletting, the self-mortification techniques required for the Maya Vision Quest were severe: the penis was cut or pierced with cords linked to other participants; the tongue was punctured and long cords or sticks "the size of a thumb" passed through the opening.'

Modern Primitives, and the subculture it promoted, focuses on exotic foreign rites, but connections between masochism and religion can be found much closer to home. In the second appendix to his 1956 study of religion *Heaven and Hell*, Aldous Huxley writes on the visionaries and mystics common to early Christianity: ' . . . most contemplatives worked systematically to modify their body chemistry, with a view to creating the internal conditions favourable to spiritual insight. When they were not starving themselves into low blood sugar and a vitamin deficiency, or beating themselves into intoxication . . . they were cultivating insomnia and praying for long periods in uncomfortable positions, in order to create the psycho-physical symptoms of stress.' In other words, Christian holymen were just as prone to masochistic extremes as their more 'primitive' equivalents.

Over 120 years later, author Brenda Love expounded on 'algophilia' (pleasure from pain) in her *Encyclopedia of Unusual Sex Practices*, as something largely born of a physiological origin rather than a purely psychological fetish: 'We detect somatic pain by stimulation of the free nerve endings that lie near the surface of the skin. Once activated they transmit a signal to the brain, however, this is not a guarantee that the sensation will be perceived as painful . . . a person's mood affects this process and if he is anxious the pain will be sharper, whereas if he is sexually aroused, feels safe, in control, and submits to the partner, the sensation may even seem pleasant . . . Extroverts are thought to require stronger tactile and mental stimulation than introverts and will not register pain as quickly. Once pain has been registered for 20-40 minutes the body will begin to produce opiate-like chemicals to reduce pain sensations. People playing with pain normally desire to create enough to trigger the release of these chemicals with their anaesthetic, euphoric and trance-like qualities . . . Modern society views pain as an affliction and does everything possible to inhibit its effects. We may someday have a better understanding of its biochemical qualities and pain may prove to have more therapeutic value for our ability to recuperate from emotional trauma than we realise.'

If religious notions are the modern fetishist's connection with the past, and the sexual psychology of pain their link to the present, then their key to the future lies in body-modification. Some modern primitives look forward to a time when we are no longer limited by the bodies we are born with and can alter them, via surgery or cybernetics, for aesthetic or pleasurable purposes. In this fetishistic utopia, the body becomes a canvas upon which we can explore limitless sexual and artistic possibilities, literally rebuilding ourselves to please ourselves. Bodily parts can be artificially decorated, enhanced, or even replaced like designer accessories. This attitude echoes (albeit darkly) in the *Mechanical Animals* that are the focus of Marilyn Manson's third album, and harks back to the nineteenth-century Decadents who believed the artificial to be superior to the natural (as in Huysmans' *Against Nature*).

It's a short leap from the Decadent ideal of man modelling his environment to suit his own tastes to the concept of an individual modelling their own flesh to the same ends. In his book *Moral Ruins*, editor Brian Stableford observes, 'If one can speak at all about a Decadent Ideal World . . . then the ideal world would be a world in which people had total control over all matters of biology, including their own anatomy, physiology and physical desires; it is an ideal which we can and ought to share, though far too few of us actually do.'

There has always been a heavily sexual element in rock'n'roll, even before the provocative wiggle in Elvis's pelvis outraged conservative America in the 1950s. Indeed, the very term is derived from black slang for sex. The relationship between a performer and their audience obviously has sexual roots, and it's difficult to describe the hysteria caused by popular bands among teenage girls as anything other than some strange emotional orgasm-by-proxy. Typically, Marilyn Manson have their own version of this sexual relationship between performer and audience, deliberately bringing its abusive aspects to the fore, and there are times when their tours seem more like travelling sadomasochistic orgies than roadshows.

Early Manson shows, which were in many ways provocative pieces of performance art, featured the frontman leading Nancy (later to form an abusive relationship with the singer) to the stage on a leash. He recalls the onstage relationship's rapid descent into depravity, beginning with Nancy's suggestion that he punch her in the face. The physical abuse became progressively crueller, to the point where Marilyn later speculated as to whether it may have caused 'some brain damage because she began falling in love with me . . . Nancy and I began exploring sexuality as well as pain and dominance onstage.'

Success saw Marilyn Manson take their Theatre of Abuse from the intimacy of Florida clubs to larger venues. 'There's a real connection between the audience and us,' Manson observes, 'and it's a powerful energy that can be directed in any form, whether it's sexual or violent. It goes according to what people want.' The sadomasochistic element is overt, from the exchanges of spitting to Marilyn's self-mutilation and attacks upon other band members. 'Everyone's going to get something different out of it. At our shows, it seems, people don't know whether to fuck each other or kill each other, and hopefully the same goes for listening to the record.' And the religious overtones of his acts of self-mutilation are not unconscious. 'It was a bit symbolic, on one level, because in front of an audience I see it as being ritualistic,' says Manson, recognising the practice as 'very old and powerful'.

Marilyn Manson bring this same sadomasochistic atmosphere to their backstage activities, where conventional rock'n'roll promiscuity gives way to more exotically dangerous indulgences. *The Long Hard Road Out of Hell* documents the sadomasochistic relationship between performer and fan pursued at a more intimate level. Under the influence of their irrepressible roadie Tony Wiggins, the band developed a routine that subjected hapless female fans to an experience somewhere between bondage sex, a religious confessional and a brutal session of psychotherapy.

The determination to bring this same sadomasochistic edge to Marilyn Manson's records led the band to record one such session at the start of the *Smells Like Children* EP. The record label vetoed its inclusion, but Marilyn describes the episode vividly in his autobiography. The girl demanded humiliation and abuse, and Wiggins – his partner in debauchery – obliged. The girl's pubic hair is cut off, she is whipped, and a chain wrapped 'ominously around her neck'. It's still not enough, and the session degenerates into a vortex of sadomasochism which climaxes with the girl screaming that's she's worthless, and wants to be killed. Even a veteran of degradation like Wiggins is shaken by this, and tries to make sure his victim's okay – 'she let loose a flurry of screams that no longer differentiated between pleasure and pain. "You know I'm not going to kill you," he tried to soothe her. "I don't fucking care," she told him. "This feels so fucking good."'

This same sadomasochistic ethos has been expressed throughout Marilyn Manson's

THE UNKINDEST CUT

Self-mutilating wild-man Iggy Pop.

Perhaps the most unsettling aspects of Marilyn Manson's stageshow – the parts that give even his most cynical critics pause for thought – are those moments when he cuts himself using broken bottles, or whatever else comes to hand. It became a regular feature during the band's 1995 tour with Danzig, where the vocalist began in earnest to chart what he calls 'the road map across my chest'. On the surface, self-mutilation seemed to reflect exhaustion and disillusionment caused by the strain of endless touring. Beneath that, as Marilyn confessed: 'I was deep in the cavity of misery because Missi had called and said she wanted to end our relationship – the first relationship that meant anything to me'.

Marilyn Manson isn't the first rock star to publicly carve his frustrations into his torso. Back in the early 1970s, Iggy Pop's taunting of his audience turned self-destructively bloody as he got increasingly deeper into violent self-mutilation (also apparently originating from woman trouble, though drug abuse and general psychosis began to play their parts). This kind of extreme behaviour has a long and curious tradition in the entertainment world. Early twentieth-century American opera singer Geraldine Farrar once revealed to an interviewer that at every performance she cut herself open with a knife. According to Brenda Love in *The Encyclopedia of Unusual Sexual Practices*, 'Cutting creates an intense moment and display of personal power over the person's fate. The person's cicatrix acts as a constant affirmation of their new found power over pain and tragedy.'

career. 'You can't make art without pain,' their frontman opines. 'Without sex, dope, confusion or whatever. You can't grasp good music just out of air. You must do something for it. You must find yourself in your music. If not, it is just nothing.'

Nowhere is this more evident than on *Antichrist Superstar*, which he describes as akin to an occult ritual. Central to that ritual was the abuse and pain the band subjected themselves to during its recording, a series of ordeals close to the sacred masochism of the modern primitive subculture. 'I would put myself through a lot of physical pain with drugs or masochistic behaviour,' Marilyn recalls. 'And that was something that transformed me, really. I find myself being a different person. Yet no therapy was involved. I've tried a couple of times, but I find that self-examination works better for me than trying to explain it to someone else'. Like the modern primitives, he discovered his personal spirituality in the altered states brought about by suffering and sleep-deprivation, but, like Anton LaVey, he identified the 'satanic' power of those states as lying somewhere between religion and psychiatry.

There is an unquestionable authenticity about Marilyn Manson's fixation with the dark side of the libido. When he says, 'To me, sex was ugly and still is – about fucking pigs and putting douche bags up your ass,' you are inclined to believe this dedication to deviance is sincere (in spirit, if not in deed). If Sigmund Freud is to be believed, we must look to the experiences of the young Brian Warner for the origin of this attitude. In *The Encyclopedia of Unusual Sexual Practices*, Brenda Love has this to say on masochism:

'The reason people feel a need to convey love in this manner often lies in their past environmental conditioning . . . In addition, these people probably only received nurturing from their parents when they were ill or injured, therefore, they may feel that the only time they are permitted to receive nurturing is when they are weak or injured. Similar conditioning is now considered a contributing factor for people who become sexually aroused by piercing and cutting . . . Masochism plays a role in creating a feeling of self empowerment or self esteem. The masochist faces fear, pain, or humiliation and not only survives but has an orgasm or receives love as a reward.'

In his autobiography, Marilyn describes a claustrophobic childhood relationship with his mother wherein she tried to maintain the bond by convincing her son he was more sickly than he actually was. Brian Warner's early life is crowded with incidents where sex, pain, perversion and spirituality become hopelessly entangled. The pious teacher at the Christian Heritage School who most fills him with loathing also inspires lust, tormenting the young boy with a confused blend of hatred and longing. Picking the favourite article from his early journalistic career to reproduce in *The Long Hard Road Out of Hell*, he would choose 'We Always Hurt the Ones We Love'. It was a feature about Mistress Barbara – a 'short, corpulent' dominatrix who 'represents everything a woman is about while at the same time contradicting what we believe is normal behaviour'.

Sometimes, emotion cuts much deeper than any flesh wound inflicted by a dominatrix, as Marilyn soon learned. His autobiography records an unhappy relationship with a girl named Rachelle, whose betrayal inflicts emotional pain on him that makes Mistress Barbara's activities look tame by comparison. (He cites this romantic trauma as central in his decision to emotionally distance himself from a world he regarded with increasing distrust.) Manson even describes his pivotal professional relationship with Trent Reznor in sadomasochistic terms, claiming it was like Miss Barbara's Dungeon, 'strewn with unforseeable peaks of pleasure and pain'.

Such frustrations would erupt in Marilyn Manson performances, which became notorious for the lead singer's habit of cutting himself on stage. While touring with Danzig, Marilyn performed his first major act of public self-mutilation, inspired by the apathy and antipathy of the crowd. In a fit of rage, he seized a beer bottle, smashed it on the drum kit, then bellowed a challenge at the crowd, stunning them and the band into virtual silence. There were no takers, so Manson carved the bottle across his own chest, creating what he describes as 'one of the deepest and biggest scars on the latticework that is my torso'. From thereon in, the gigs transformed from tour dates to confrontational exercises in drug-fuelled performance art, while 'the road map across my chest began to expand with scars, bruises and welts. We had all become wretched, exhausted, empty containers . . .'

As Brenda Love observes of this kind of self-mutilation (which she calls cicatrization), 'Cutting has always been a basis for emotional healing. Today many people in mental institutions, hospitals, and prisons engage in cutting as a form of self-mutilation. The reasons given for this kind of behaviour vary, but most feel it puts them back in touch with their bodies so they feel human again.'

At bottom, the primary origin of fetishism remains the expression of individuality – which is why the fetish counterculture finds its darkest high-profile advocate in Marilyn Manson, the self-appointed 'Nineties voice of individuality'. Recalling the surreptitious childhood visit to his grandfather's deviant den, in 1996 the newly-transformed Antichrist returned to his family home in Canton, Ohio, feeling drawn back to the cellar where the old man had kept all of his guilty sexual secrets. There Marilyn came face-to-face with what he himself had become.

The cellar is no longer a place of dread. On the contrary, it's now the only place in his childhood hometown where he really feels secure. He even feels more in common with his grandfather than the young Brian Warner – like Grandfather Jack Marilyn Manson wears women's lingerie, while his career of perversity makes the tawdry magazines and photos hidden in his grandfather's dingy lair look tame by comparison. 'My grandfather had been the ugliest, darkest, foulest, most depraved figure of my childhood, more beast than human, and I had grown up to be him, locked in the basement with my secrets as the rest of the family revelled in the petty and ordinary upstairs.'

If little Brian Warner, like his grandfather, had given way to dark appetites as he grew up, then at least they were his *own* appetites – not the sanitised demands of Church or TV. Rather than sacrificing your individuality, sometimes, perhaps, it's better to be a deviant or a monster.

Chapter Seven

THE FASCIST FREAKSHOW

With serial murder, sadomasochism and child abuse (metaphorically) under his belt, some wondered which taboos, if any, Marilyn Manson had left to break. Their answer came in 1996 with the Dead to the World tour, promoting *Antichrist Superstar*. In a show packed with melodrama, the most theatrical moment featured banners bearing the Antichrist 'shock symbol' and the besuited frontman strutting like some political rabble-rouser or charismatic evangelist. Lights and music pumped in militaristic rhythm as Marilyn Manson, Reverend of the Church of Satan, mounted the pulpit, encouraging the audience to punch the air in time. The gesture looked suspiciously close to a Nazi salute, the whole show beginning to resemble a fascist rally more than a rock concert. It was no accident.

Perhaps it was only a matter of time before Marilyn Manson, with his self-confessed desire to become America's biggest villain, would invoke the closest thing to the Devil the twentieth century has seen: Adolf Hitler. The huge suffering associated with the rise and fall of Hitler's Third Reich makes fascism one of the biggest taboos of the modern world, unable to be discussed except in the most condemnatory terms. Of course, this didn't stop Marilyn from airing the Western world's dirtiest political laundry. 'A lot of people were afraid for me to do it,' he noted. 'But I felt if I did it well enough, people would understand what I was getting at. In the end, it caused all the different reactions that I wanted. Some people thought it was great satire, others thought I was a fascist, others just blindly pumped their fists and didn't notice the irony.'

Even in a spirit of irony, however, fascism is an extremely sensitive topic to address. 'There will always be misconceptions,' its creator had observed of the reactions to *Antichrist Superstar*, 'people will misconceive this record as being purely evil, either Satanic or fascist. But it's so hard to put it into any of those terms because it's extreme. It's positive and negative in its purest form.' He could hardly pretend, however, that he hadn't invited such assumptions, via the imagery and symbols utilised on the album and accompanying tour.

ROCKING THE SWASTIKA

Swastikas swiftly became part of punk's uniform of outrage.

Marilyn Manson are far from the first band whose flirtation with fascist imagery has inspired outrage from the media. While obscure punk-metal-skinhead groups like the UK's Skrewdriver, or America's Rahowa (abbreviated from 'racial holy war'), are authentic members of a racist underground, most performers who have invoked the spirit of the Nazis have done so as a cheap shock tactic, or in an ironic tone. As early as the 1960s, Brian Jones of the Rolling Stones was courting controversy by posing for photographs in an SS uniform. Keith Moon of the Who and Vivian Stanshall of psychedelic satirists the Bonzo Dog Band aspired to the ultimate in bad taste, cavorting in Nazi regalia through the predominantly Jewish area of Golders Green in London. Pugnacious theatrical Scots rocker Alex Harvey – though an early supporter of Rock Against Racism – was prone to dressing up as Hitler, going so far as to hold a 'Nazi party' in 1975 where guests were expected to attend in appropriate costume.

In the early days of punk, Siouxsie infamously appeared at a Sex Pistols concert wearing a swastika armband and not much else. Some of the early goth bands who emerged in her wake also used ideas and images evoking the horrors of the Third Reich: Joy Division were named after a squad of female concentration camp inmates forced to prostitute themselves to the SS. Spear of Destiny took their name from a myth (touted as fact in a best-selling book) that the Nazis had tried to harness the occult power of the spear that pierced Christ's side on the cross. New Order, the band formed from the ashes of Joy Division, denied their name was taken from the new world order promised by Hitler after the victory of the Third Reich; less ambiguously, *the New Order*, a late-seventies metal-punk band formed by an ex-member of the Stooges, were inspired in their choice of name by a fascination for Nazi memorabilia. Heavy metal bands have been traditionally pragmatic in their interest in Nazism, toying with the iron crosses and military imagery but ignoring the political dimensions (Lemmy of Motorhead and Pete Steele of Type O Negative are both collectors of Nazi militaria).

The artist whose brief flirtation with fascism caused the most consternation was David Bowie. In his incarnation as the 'Thin White Duke', Bowie adopted an aristocratic European image which many thought smacked of fascism. It was an impression compounded by a 1976 interview when, as Marilyn Manson later would, he drew comparisons between the charisma of a rock star and a political dictator. Bowie opined that he 'could have been a bloody good Hitler in England – it wouldn't have been hard ... I'd be an excellent dictator. Very eccentric and quite mad.' While these comments can be dismissed as flippancy, others sound alarmingly sincere. 'I'd adore to be Prime Minister,' claimed the singer. 'And, yes, I believe very strongly in fascism . . . People have always responded with greater efficiency under a regimental leadership.' He even referred to Hitler as 'the first rock star', for having 'staged a nation'.

Challenged on these comments by a Swedish journalist, Bowie brazenly replied, 'I am the only alternative for the premiere in England. I believe Britain could benefit from a fascist leadership. After all, fascism is really nationalism.' Things went from bad to worse when, on a British tour promoting his *Station to Station* album – with stage lighting based on that created by Albert Speer for Hitler's Nuremberg rallies – Bowie was photographed greeting his fans with what looked like a Nazi salute.

This bizarre episode proved to be a sinister blip in the singer's brilliant but erratic career. As he would later explain, his twin Nazi/occult obsession was fuelled by megalomania and cocaine psychosis, with no basis in racism. (He continued to play r'n'b-based music, mix with people of all races and date black women, and was the first white artist to appear on *Soul Train*, all during his 'fascist' period.) By the time he left Los Angeles for Berlin, abandoning the lifestyle that threatened to destroy him, any suspicions that his new city of choice had some ideological basis were a clear embarrassment to him.

'Fascist' is a term often used as an insult but seldom fully understood. The popular conception of fascism is as a label for extreme racism and violently oppressive tyranny. In the modern world, those who subscribe to such a doctrine are usually out to make an anti-social statement, often born of frustration, and neo-Nazi fringe groups are small in number and importance.

Technically speaking, 'fascism' only describes a form of government where everything is subordinated to the demands of the state. Concerns like personal liberty, individual rights and commercial freedom are secondary to the interests of the nation, as determined by the leadership. Nationalistic and patriotic by nature, fascism demands strong leaders – though it doesn't inevitably imply dictatorship by a single man. Neither inherently good nor evil, the single-mindedness of the fascist state makes it more efficient in achieving its aims, but has no checks on its behaviour should those aims become twisted or pathological.

Perversely, despite its aura of violence and repression, fascism sometimes sneaks in through the backdoor of popular politics rather than as a result of violent *coup d'etat*. Hitler's attempt at taking power by force was a disaster – only when he resorted to the ballot box did he establish his grip on power in Germany, winning by a small mandate and banning democratic elections soon after.

Fascism's view of the world is almost romantic, emphasising heroism, struggle and national tradition. In this sense, the fascist values honour above compassion, and duty above personal freedom, with a tendency to see the world in mythic terms and few compunctions about sacrifices made (often by unwilling parties) in the name of his great crusade. The past is a glorious heritage and the future an epic destiny.

Just as Satanism was born as a reaction to Christianity, so fascism was born as a reaction to left-wing egalitarianism and communism. Its roots are in the late eighteenth century when Europe was shaken by a series of rebellions, most notably the French Revolution of 1789. Across Europe, many Romantic writers and artists were initially excited by events and hailed the Revolution as a triumph for liberty. But as the revolutionaries' idealism turned to bloodlust, admiration turned to disgust among the Romantics. Just as the ideals of fascism are associated with the Holocaust today, so the ideals of government by the people were haunted by the spectre of the guillotine back then. It became clear that if the *Ancien Régime* (the old, corrupt aristocratic system) was to be overthrown, it had to be by something nobler, purer, more heroic than the mobs that overran Paris. So the seeds of romantic fascism were planted – a system based not upon government by the masses or a hereditary aristocracy, but on heroic leadership.

Europe's *Ancien Régime*, teetering for centuries, finally toppled as the First World War destroyed an entire generation of Europe's young men, and any faith in the political systems that started the mindless, bloody mess. In Russia that dissatisfaction boiled over into the October Revolution of 1917, as workers and soldiers took a violent revenge on their aristocratic leaders which resulted in the first communist state. Across Europe, fascism grew in response to the perceived threat of this selfsame workers' revolution. In Italy, the first fascist party was founded in 1919 by Benito Mussolini, who coined the term after the Ancient Roman 'fasces' – a bundle of sticks bound around an axe to symbolise the power of a united purpose. The Italian fascists contrasted the left-wing revolutionary maxim of 'liberty, equality, fraternity' with their own doctrine of 'believe, obey, fight', Mussolini seizing power in 1922.

In Germany, the National Socialist Party (usually abbreviated to the more familiar 'Nazis') was founded in 1920, with Adolf Hitler taking over the leadership the following year. The Nazi party grew from the chaos of Germany after its disastrous defeat in the First World War, when a humiliated nation was looking for strong leadership and scapegoats. With the Jews as scapegoats and Hitler elected as Germany's fascist leader in 1933, the rest, as cliché has it, is history.

While the rabid anti-Semitism of the Nazis is well known, their hatred of 'decadence' is not so often remembered. They didn't just want racial purity, but also cultural and artistic purity, and were repelled by the scandalously decadent subculture of 1920s Berlin. This puritanical attitude was very popular with the voters, boosting the narrow margin that brought them to power.

In the modern popular consciousness, the Nazis and the decadent culture they opposed have become confused. The SS officer, with his monocle and black leather riding boots, has been transformed into a decadent figure familiar to all popular fetish clubs – partly due to the unhealthy idea that, as the twentieth century's most infamous oppressors, Nazis make good models for the recreational sadist. Susan Sontag made a detailed study of this sinister idea in *Under the Sign of Saturn*, in which she writes: 'Between sadomasochism and fascism there is a natural link. Fascism is theatre . . . as is sadomasochistic sexuality . . . expert costumers and choreographers as well as performers, in a drama that is all the more exciting because it is forbidden to ordinary people.'

The Nazis as an icon of erotic fascination have much to do with their sense of visual drama. As conservative American humorist P. J. O'Rourke puts it, 'I've often been called a Nazi, and, although it is unfair, I don't let it bother me for one simple reason. No one has *ever* had a fantasy about being tied to a bed and sexually ravished by someone dressed as a liberal.' From an amoral viewpoint, if you're looking for an archetype of absolute power to employ in your sadomasochistic sex games, few fit the bill better than the Nazis, the twentieth century's ultimate authoritarian control freaks. But the appeal also lies in fantasies of the 'forbidden', reinventing them as deliciously dangerous deviants rather than the pleasure-hating puritans they really were.

Many of those who promote the confusion between Nazism and decadence are puritans who want to rewrite history, associating the horrors of the Holocaust with unbridled freedom rather than repression. In the wake of the shootings at Columbine High School, the media similarly tried to lay the blame on Marilyn Manson by laying a campaign of cynical misinformation. In reality, research by more conscientious journalists revealed that the two teenagers responsible hated the decadent 'faggot' Marilyn, while idolising Adolf Hitler as an anti-social icon. Any statement the teenage misfits were trying to make remains incoherent – ironically, Hitler would almost certainly have sided with the healthy Aryan 'jocks' targeted by the pair, rather than the social outcasts the jocks had been persecuting.

Scapegoating, irony and hypocrisy – topics Marilyn Manson loves to play with – loomed large over the Columbine controversy. The National Rifle Association were quick to try to move debate away from gun control. Their most prominent spokesman, actor Charlton Heston, opined that 'Schools are responsible not to let kids like these wear black trenchcoats and funny hats, as children do all over the country' – teenage fashion obviously being the real life-or-death issue. Marilyn Manson cancelled an upcoming Denver concert, while the NRA's planned Denver conference went ahead. The reactionary press began a witch-hunt against 'rock freak' Marilyn. The UK's most popular tabloid, *The Sun*, began a crusade, instructing its readers that 'As a mark of respect to the Denver dead don't buy his [Marilyn's] records', while other papers ran Manson rumours – such as the ludicrous suggestion that he had breast implants – as 'facts' in their profiles of the singer.

While keen to point the finger at a mythical, Hitler-worshipping, gothic cult led by Marilyn Manson, the irony of their own witch-hunt was evidently lost on most journalists. If any single phenomenon (apart from the mental state of the perpetrators) can be held accountable for the Columbine massacre, it's the persecution of young social misfits by their peers. The international print media took that same persecution of non-conformity to new levels in their coverage of the tragedy. Even supposedly liberal papers like the UK's *Observer* began pointing the finger at some imaginary evil counterculture, quoting 'anti-Satanism expert' Professor Carl Raschke who blamed Columbine on 'a pop outgrowth of the decadent and occult movements of the last century in France, Germany and England, which formed the basis for Nazism'.

While Raschke's assertion is pure hysteria, it has to be admitted that there is a relationship between decadence and romantic fascism – they share the same parentage. This cultural Cain and Abel are both born of nihilism, the belief in nothing. Nihilism is the result of everything you regarded as worthwhile or significant ultimately appearing to be illusory or worthless. In cultural terms, this usually means losing faith in both God and government, often after a defeat in war and the wastage of human life that seems so pointless with hindsight. Nihilism, being by definition a state of emptiness, cannot last, and will lead down either one of two roads.

If everything is going to hell and nothing really matters, we might as well enjoy ourselves and forget the rules and ethics we now know to be meaningless – hence decadence. Or we may try to replace the values we have lost by creating a new, greater, stronger icon to bow down before, imposing rules and ideals so ruthlessly rigid they

MONKEY MAN

The man who did the most damage to Christianity during the nineteenth century was also one of its most reluctant opponents. Charles Darwin only published his masterpiece, *On the Origin of Species by Means of Natural Selection*, in 1859 because he feared another scientist was about to publish similar conclusions. His theory hit contemporary society like a thunderbolt, the book selling out on the day of publication and sparking heated debate across Europe. Darwin was not the first to suggest that animals had not been created by God, but had evolved from more primitive species via the process of natural selection – but he was the first to present the theory so convincingly. His fiercest opponents were clergymen who recognised that his challenge to the story of Creation, as told in the Book of Genesis, invited a wholesale dismissal of *The Bible* as a work of fiction.

Darwin's theory of natural selection stresses that creatures best suited to survival are more likely to keep breeding, propagating their species. By a process of evolutionary mutation, certain creatures become dominant while others die out – later labelled 'survival of the fittest'. It's a measure of the importance of Darwin that many Christians still choose this area – evolutionary theory, opposed to their own primitive 'creationism' – as a battleground for their rearguard action against the advance of rationalism. Most intelligent people, however, now accept Darwin's theory in some form.

But debate continues to rage. Darwin himself was aware of the volatile potential of applying his theory to human beings, restraining himself to one sentence in *The Origin of the Species* that reads, 'Light will be thrown on the origin of man and his history.' Most controversial of all is the concept of Social Darwinism: the idea that the merciless law of survival of the fittest applies not only to the animal world, but also to human society. This line of thinking led to the science of eugenics, where attempts were made to 'aid' natural selection by artificially improving the quality of the population. Eugenics was widely discredited after the Second World War, when Nazi breeding programs and extermination camps were exposed as the grotesque extreme of Social Darwinism.

cannot be destroyed — in other words, fascism. Ironically, the second, more positive-sounding route leads us to the death camps — while the first, which smacks of wickedness, has left us with some very beautiful poetry and exciting rock music.

Just as a rejection of all previous values can occur within a culture, as in Germany after the First World War, so it can occur within individuals. The iconoclastic German philosopher Friedrich Nietzsche was concerned with the struggle of the individual to escape nihilism and transcend the temptations of decadence. His answer lay in the 'will to power' — the quest to overcome your own weaknesses and evolve into something more than human, the *übermensch* or, more crudely, the 'superman'. If this sounds like fascism to you, you're not alone — the Nazis adopted Nietzsche (who died in 1900) as their favoured philosopher. While this association with the Third Reich makes him an obviously controversial figure, his modern admirers are quick to point out that the struggle Nietzsche described was an internal battle with the self, not an armed conflict that would engulf half the globe. (Had Nietzsche survived far into the twentieth century, most of his admirers now claim he would have resisted the Nazi appropriation of his ideas, which was facilitated by his anti-Semitic sister.)

Among these admirers is Marilyn Manson, who regularly quotes and paraphrases the nineteenth-century philosopher. In fact, Marilyn's career can be seen as an exploration of the process described above: nihilism (the breakdown of American values in *Portrait of an American Family*) is followed by a flirtation with fascism (*Antichrist Superstar*) and an exploration of decadence (*Mechanical Animals*). Of these, *Antichrist Superstar* evokes the spirit of Nietzsche most powerfully. In Nietzsche's 1888 essay attacking Christianity, *The Antichrist*, he used the word as Marilyn Manson later would, to mean an enemy of Christianity (as opposed to the demonic anti-messiah of medieval myth). 'I consider it to be a record about individuality and personal strength,' the Nietzschean rock star said of *Antichrist Superstar*, 'putting yourself through a lot of temptations and torments, seeing your own death and growing from it.'

Marilyn waxed explicit on the impact of Nietzsche on his life and work during promotional interviews for the album: 'It's like the superman theory that Nietzsche had, I think every man and woman is a star. It's just a matter of realising it and becoming it. It's all a matter of willpower. You know, the world is just how you see it. If you want to have other people tell you how you see it, then you can. But if you want to look at it, then it's limitless what you can do. That's why I don't feel the need to ever have to be one person. I can be as many different people as I like. It's a matter of "should you follow the rules that the world has set up for you?" or "should you make your own?" I choose to make my own.'

Nietzsche is not the only philosopher invoked here. 'Every Man and Every Woman is a Star' (an idea which contradicts the whole Nietzschean ethos) is taken from Aleister Crowley's *Book of the Law*, and is one of the less disturbing doctrines in Crowley's often

Beyond Good and Evil

A translation of Nietzsche's The Antichrist *issued by controversial author and maverick musician Michael Moynihan.*

Freidrich Nietzsche remains perhaps the most controversially fascinating philosopher of all time. Born in Prussia in 1844, his difficult life is reflected in his bleak, bold view of the world. Possessed of a brilliant intellect, dogged by ill health (syphilis took a progressive toll throughout his life) and romantic disappointment, he attempted to find meaning in the face of a universe that seemed cruel and arbitrary. This struggle precipitated his mental breakdown in 1889, and quite probably his death in 1900, but left a canon of books outlining, in prose-poem form, a philosophy whose influence has grown throughout the twentieth century. To some, Nietzsche represents the ultimate rugged individualist, a hero who dared face up to what it really means to be human. To others, his story is a tragedy illustrating the dangers of enshrining the ego, in what one Christian critic described as a 'philosophy of madness'.

'God is dead!' Nietzsche declared, distilling the feeling that was beginning to dawn on many people in the nineteenth century, a realisation that the power of religion was collapsing under the weight of science and reason. What's more, he believed the Christian God deserved his symbolic extinction at the hands of his human creators, and that the Almighty was a 'slave god' who appealed to humanity's tendencies toward cowardice, stupidity and conformity. However, the German philosopher recognised that the destruction of traditional values like religion created a dangerous void, an abyss. To fill this void Nietzsche preached that man needed to evolve into a higher form – a stronger, wiser, more sensitive state achieved through sheer force of will. He called this new heroic figure the 'übermensch' ('overman', or superman).

This painful struggle to evolve is at the heart of Nietzsche's philosophy. It replaces traditional ideas of good and evil with the opposition between the individual with the potential to evolve and the great mass of humanity whose envy and ignorance hamper the process. In this conflict, the übermensch is not subject to the same rules and moral boundaries as ordinary mortals. One century after his death, Nietzsche's stature continues to grow, though controversy over this brilliant, tragic figure's philosophy shows no signs of abating.

merciless religion, which, like Nietzsche, described the world in terms of masters and slaves, regarding the Christian god as personifying the slave mentality. Crowley, the Great Beast, saw himself as the herald of the death of the Christian slave god, and the start of a new, exciting aeon of 'Do what thou wilt'. The beginning of the new aeon would be marked by great bloodshed and chaos – some interpreting this as the First World War, though, in terms of sheer cruelty, it was a mere rehearsal for the conflict Hitler would launch in 1939.

There are parallels between Crowleyanity and National Socialism – both being creeds of mystical elitism – which make Crowley's (largely left-wing or liberal) modern disciples distinctly uncomfortable. The Great Beast, like Hitler, was anti-Semitic in attitude and dictatorial in character, and both men believed in the importance of the will. (As does Crowley's illustrious disciple, Marilyn Manson, who once claimed, 'Sheer willpower over talent can get you what you want. I've proved to people that doubted me that I do have talent, but what got me here is my willpower, my determination. That can apply to anybody in any part of their lives. It doesn't have to be music, it can be any sort of expression.')

The widest early acceptance of *The Book of the Law* had been among the German-based occult movement the Ordo Templi Orientis, whose leadership Crowley would later assume. Some of his German disciples saw connections between Crowleyanity and Nazism, notably an occultist named Martha Küntzel. In his unsympathetic biography of Crowley, *The King of the Shadow Realm*, John Symonds writes that 'she loved Hitler as much as she did Crowley. To her mind, the two leaders, one of a nation, the other of a mystical society, were working to the same end, that of establishing a new world order based on the true will. In 1925, Crowley told her that the nation which first adopted *The Book of the Law* would become the leading nation of the world. According to the Beast, Martha Küntzel thought that the then insignificant Adolf Hitler, who had received a setback after his failed Munich putsch in 1923, was Germany's coming man; so she sent him, again according to Crowley, a copy of her translation of *Liber Legis* [*The Book of the Law*]. In her eyes, the Master Therion [Crowley] was the prophet of National Socialism.'

Despite this, the Nazis pursued an active policy of persecuting occultists, particularly those associated with the decadent Crowley, and a number of his most important German disciples ended up in concentration camps. Even Küntzel, that fervent admirer of Hitler, had her papers seized and destroyed by the Nazi authorities. Nevertheless, the myth endures of the Third Reich as a kind of demonic dictatorship, a *Raiders of the Lost Ark*-style fantasy. The Nazis have become confused both with the decadence they hated, and the occultists they reviled and persecuted.

By the time Marilyn Manson assimilated the imagery of fascism, the stageshow resembled a religious sermon as much as a Far Right rally. The deliberate subtext – highlighting the quasi-fascist implications of Christianity's tradition of violent repression and demands for unconditional loyalty – was too close to the bone for many evangelical Christians. It was redolent of the fact that Hitler, who has been posthumously compared to Satan, actually cast himself in the role of Christ, as did his 'disciples'.

'The part of the show where I stand at the podium and I have the banners come down,' described Marilyn, 'I'm mocking Christianity and simultaneously mocking myself, mocking a rock show, and people are cheering and pumping their fists to it – that in itself is just a great statement. Whether anyone understands it at all, it doesn't matter.'

The similarities between the group hysteria, and mindless adulation, of a rock concert and the emotional manipulation of crowds at Hitler's Nuremberg Rallies are also parodied. 'There's definitely ritual in music,' Marilyn observes, 'it just depends if artists are smart enough to use it or not. Anything from a sporting event to a totalitarian rally to a rock concert has a lot of energy, which can be either chaotic or focused. When you focus it, it has a lot of power. A lot of people have learned to do that over the years for evil purposes, whether it be Julius Caesar, Stalin or Hitler. Others, whether it be me, Madonna or Elvis Presley have used it for positive things.'

Just as the relationship between rock stars and their fans (an abbreviation of 'fanatics') is often deeply sexual in nature, so there are erotic, perhaps sadomasochistic elements in the adoration some crowd members feel for dictators. Albert Speer, architect and minister of the Third Reich, identified that element in Hitler's legendary speeches: 'It was not so much what he said – I hardly remembered afterwards – but the mood he cast over the entire hall: it had an almost orgiastic quality. Hitler always said that the masses are essentially feminine, and his aggressiveness and charisma elicited an almost masochistic surrender and submission in his audience – a form of psychic rape.'

Even among those who understood Marilyn Manson's use of fascist imagery, however, there was some disquiet. Some felt it was unforgivably tasteless to invoke fascism in the entertainment arena, or that 'psychically raping' audiences with the tactics of a dictator could be addictive – that Marilyn was somehow in danger of becoming what he parodied. It was a delicious irony, not wasted on the Antichrist Superstar who played with it in interview after interview. Could a rock concert, essentially a venue for the mob psychology at the heart of fascism, ever really be said to promote individualism?

'*Antichrist Superstar* examined that on a lot of different levels,' affirmed Marilyn. 'It even examined the herd mentality of rock'n'roll. And I think by looking at that, it made all of us smarter. It made the fans smarter. It made me smarter. I think it gave us all the perspective to realise that Christianity and rock'n'roll are very similar in a sense, and if you can see that, you can point out your own hypocrisy. Then you can go above it and you can try and be "realer" than anything else.'

Fascism may be inherent in the music industry. Like most creative pursuits, making music rarely works well if everyone has equal input, and is usually better directed by a single vision. Most great bands are dictatorships, not democracies. 'It's easy to hate a dictator if you're not him,' Marilyn has observed. 'But if you are him, I'm sure it's great . . . I'm an absolute dictator within the band. You can't trust a bunch of guys to try and decide where they're gonna go – you have to tell them.'

If 'fascism', in its bastardised sense, is defined as a policy of strict conformity, then it's pretty much everywhere. The hippies, who made a habit of labelling their opponents 'fascists' in the 1960s, were just as rigid in conforming to their counterculture as the 'squares' were in adhering to mainstream culture. By the 1980s the flower children had come of age, many taking jobs where they could impose what became known as 'political correctness' from within the system. In the 1990s, Marilyn Manson would attack such 'compassion fascism' with as much vigour as its right-wing equivalent.

POLITICALLY INCORRECT

Not content with upsetting conservative bigots, tearing up Bibles and wiping his ass on the American flag, Marilyn Manson is just as eager to stir up trouble among the liberal left. The band's cover of the Patti Smith song 'rock'n'roll Nigger' has been misinterpreted (perhaps deliberately) as racist, with municipal authorities pressurising them to remove it from their set more than once. (Smith's song uses the word 'nigger' in the tradition of Norman Mailer's 'White Nigger', and is inspired in part by the French decadent poet Arthur Rimbaud.) More controversially, Manson have also covered 'One in a Million' by Guns 'n' Roses, a track which caused a storm of outrage in 1988 for its off-colour comments about foreigners and homosexuals: 'Immigrants and faggots, they make no sense to me/They come to our country and spread some fucking disease.'

'It's interesting to me that Axl Rose would write a song like that and then back down in the press and not be able to defend his statement,' said the eponymous frontman. 'If you're going to have the balls to make that kind of statement, then you should be able to back it up. So I figure I'll say it and then show him how it's done properly. These people really don't know how to do anything right! I have to take up all their slack for them. I'm not doing it because I agree with their statements, but because someone needs to do it properly.'

PARENTAL ADVISORY EXPLICIT CONTENT

'Well, now it's just the same like at the end of the sixties,' he observed, 'everywhere you went, you were pumped up with messages that made being yourself out to be a sin. "You must recycle, don't smoke in public places, be friendly to your neighbours, don't be sexist and a racist" and this and that . . . And people are so shy when they want to say what they feel. They don't tell a girl how beautiful she is. It could be sexist or they don't want to say they hate a black or white man, because he is an asshole – the neighbours could say you're a racist. These are things which are going into your mind through television and newspapers and such things. You can't see them but you know what they do! A crazy, hidden fascism. There isn't a big brother who controls all, but many, many little brothers who observe all who don't fit in the morality.'

So what does he advocate as an alternative to the public's mindless conformity? Suggesting a positive side to the dictatorial character at the heart of *Antichrist Superstar*, Marilyn noted that 'with commercialism and television, everything's completely dictated to you, and if you don't fit into the status quo, you're made to feel you're not as good as everyone else. The type of totalitarianism that *Antichrist Superstar* suggests is a group of non-joiners, a crowd of individuals that are all banding together to change what the mainstream is. It actually can't even be described with an "ism", because I think it's above and beyond everything that's been attempted in the past. It's like a pep rally for the apocalypse.'

This was just a little disingenuous – the 'ism' in question was Satanism, as first codified in the 1960s by Anton LaVey in the Church of Satan.

SYMBOL OF SHOCK

The insignia that represents the *Antichrist Superstar* album, though it appears inherently fascistic, is just the international warning sign for high-voltage electricity. However, it has been metaphorically connected to the passage in *The Bible* where Jesus says he has seen Satan falling from Heaven like lightning. It also resembles the Church of Satan's modern-day symbol of a lightning bolt inside a pentagram, used more often today than the familiar goat's head version. Its fascistic associations are compounded by its resemblance to the 'sieg' rune, a Viking symbol meaning 'victory' that was used to form the 'S' in the SS insignia. It also echoes the insignia of Oswald Moseley's British Union of Fascists, and looks intriguingly close to the lightning make-up worn by David Bowie for the *Aladdin Sane* album cover.

The image of Nazism as an 'occult reich' is not a purely Christian myth. Some Norse pagans claim to worship the Viking gods occasionally used in Nazi propaganda, while other occultists have wholeheartedly adopted the myth of the Third Reich as a cabal of black magicians, creating a provocative axis between fascism and Satanism.

In his 1972 book *The Satanic Rituals*, Anton LaVey includes a rite called 'Die elektrischen Vorspiele', which he claims was originally performed by the Black Order – a nickname for Hitler's SS, though LaVey makes it clear he uses the term to describe the German occult lodges who existed between the wars. While he was happy to play with such incendiary doctrines, at heart the rigid conformity of the Third Reich was diametrically opposed to the Church of Satan's non-conformity. Early high-profile Church of Satan members included homosexuals like the avant-garde filmmaker Kenneth Anger, and the black-Jewish song-and-dance-man Sammy Davis, Junior, while LaVey himself had Jewish blood.

Nevertheless, racist occultists began sniffing around the Church of Satan in the 1970s. Splinter groups from LaVey's church set themselves up as fascist alternatives, renegade Ku Klux Klan chapters made overtures for affiliation, and foreign groups with neo-Nazi connections made contact, like the Anglican Church of Satan. The Black Pope responded to these overtures with polite indifference – these were people who had simply latched onto both Satan and Hitler as anti-social icons, without grasping the significance of either.

By the 1980s, however, the Church of Satan itself was dominated by a faction who flaunted fascist imagery, a new generation claiming to identify positive elements in the taboo ideology of the Far Right. Prominent among them was Boyd Rice – the musician behind the Non industrial music project – who founded the Abraxas Foundation, 'an occult fascist think tank'. (Abraxas is an obscure deity from heretical Christian lore, a god who symbolises the unification and transcendence of opposites like light and darkness, or good and evil – much like Marilyn Manson, whose very name unites apparently contradictory extremes.) Rice – a highly provocative and articulate figure who became one of the Church Of Satan's most visible representatives – would later get involved with Marilyn Manson in the band's early days, publishing interviews with them in the American rock press and receiving a 'Thank You' credit on *Portrait of an American Family*.

Boyd Rice described himself as an aesthetic rather than political fascist, clearly drawn to fascism's ruthless romanticism. It was a slap in the face to the culture of apathy and mediocrity that applauded the victim mentality – fulfilling the satanic role of cultural villain, devil's advocate. To some, the most appropriate method to achieve this during the 1980s was to put on jackboots and goosestep over the cultural landscape. For his part, Anton LaVey emphasised the powerful aesthetics of Nazism, the evocative music, striking uniforms and highly-charged rallies, stage-managed like prototypical rock concerts (a process Marilyn Manson would invert on the Dead to the World tour). This grasp of the power of symbolism was a key to the Nazis' meteoric rise to power, opined the amoral LaVey, and could be adopted without endorsing the racist ideology that came with it.

In his 1998 collection *Satan Speaks!*, the Black Pope included essays highlighting how Christians had regarded Jews as devil-worshippers, suggesting that the true Satanist's position embraced the polar opposites of Jew and Nazi: a predatory scapegoat, as in the conceptual unification of Marilyn Monroe (archetypal victim) and Charles Manson (archetypal predator).

Marilyn Manson outlines the Black Pope's position neatly, dismissing accusations that LaVey was a Nazi or a racist. Rather, the High Priest of the Church of Satan judged people according to their intelligence and, on this basis, found much of the human race wanting. Marilyn aligns himself with this fully, believing its lack of distinction in terms of class, colour or creed to be, perversely, politically correct. 'The biggest sin in Satanism is not murder, nor is it kindness,' he observes. 'It is stupidity.'

This theme of stupidity as the one true sin has been behind a number of Manson's most provocative sermons: 'I don't really have a place in my heart for stupid or weak people. There's too many people in the world, and they need to make way for the people who can actually contribute something to society.' Or, more succinctly, 'I don't think stupid people should breed.' Such pronouncements suggest a belief in eugenics – the science of attempting to improve the quality of the population by encouraging the healthy and intelligent to breed, while discouraging those considered undesirable. Once a fashionable discipline, its application by the Nazis as a policy of murder has made it a taboo topic.

Asked if he was a fascist, Marilyn Manson explained: 'I like the idea of elitism when it comes to intelligence, because that's a commodity that's available to anyone – you can learn as much as you really want to. Obviously, some people are always going to be smarter than others, some people are mentally handicapped, but to be as smart as you're capable is a fair and almost politically correct form of elitism. Fascism, when it comes to racism or sex, is too lenient. Accept all white people? There are lots of really ignorant white people I'd never consider my friend. Accepting all men wouldn't work either. But intelligence is universal and anyone can achieve it by their own willpower. That's a healthy, positive thing.'

This suggests the very crux of Marilyn Manson's political position. If, as he says here, intelligence is something universal that can be achieved by anybody, then he can afford to condemn those who choose to be stupid. But what if some people are just born naturally stupid? By suggesting their sterilisation, Marilyn himself is entering an ideological minefield where the most commonly heard insult is the word 'fascist' . . .

FASCIST

WAITING FOR THE WORM

Pink Floyd, the most popular of the progressive rock outfits that emerged from the 1960s, are not a band immediately associated with Marilyn Manson – though their influence can be heard on much of *Mechanical Animals*. (Manson mentor Anton LaVey also admired Pink Floyd: not, needless to say, for their early psychedelic music or anti-war ethos, but because of the skill with which they interwove subliminal melodies and sounds.) While Pink Floyd are best known for *The Dark Side of the Moon*, a prog-rock masterpiece that sold around twenty million copies, their grim 1979 concept album *The Wall* is more dramatically intense. In 1982, the songs were adapted into a film by director Alan Parker, starring the singer Bob Geldof (once with new-wave pop outfit the Boomtown Rats).

Pink (played by Bob Geldof) completes the transformation from rock star to fascist dictator in The Wall.

Geldof plays Pink, a rock star whose grip on reality is slipping. Haunted by an unhappy childhood, rendered almost incapable of communication by his decadent lifestyle and the strains of celebrity, Pink drifts into nightmarish fantasies. The most memorable of these are startling animations based on drawings by English satirist Gerald Scarfe, and the jaded Pink's vision of his concerts as fascist rallies. The parallels between this story and the themes of *Antichrist Superstar* and *Mechanical Animals* are striking, most notably in Marilyn Manson's evocation of Far Right rabble-rousing on the Dead to the World tour.

Chapter Eight

ANGELS OF
THE ABYSS

'Little did I know that accepting that card would be one of the most controversial things I had done to date,' wrote Marilyn Manson in his autobiography. The card in question represented his ordination as a priest of the Church of Satan, conferred by the Black Pope, Anton LaVey. 'The day I became a Satanist also happened to be the day the allied forces of Christianity and conservatism began mobilising against me.' At the same time, the newly-ordained 'Reverend' was adamant that, 'I've never been and never will be a Satan worshipper, or someone who worships the Devil.'

Elements of LaVeyan Satanism were all-pervasive in Marilyn Manson's early material: the distinctive face of LaVey appeared on newsletters and his books on recommended reading lists for Spooky Kids. LaVey's influence also manifested itself in much subtler ways. Marilyn Manson left fake dollar bills advertising his band in the street as a promotional gimmick, catching the eye and the imagination (and piquing the greed) of passers-by. The Church Of Satan had used a similar recruiting trick three decades before, leaving promotional flyers in the street that resembled dollar bills. Distinctive LaVeyan phrases peppered Marilyn's lyrics and speech during interviews – like the 'good guy badge', a term LaVey used to describe how hypocritically pious gestures hid the true self-serving nature of humanity.

For all this, Marilyn maintained, 'I don't want people to misconceive me as a spokesperson for the Church of Satan.' Was he backing off, alarmed at the vehemence of the critics who accused him of preaching Satanism? Or was he, as those confounded by his occasional approving references to the Christian *Bible* suggested, just another rock star hoping to gain credibility by associating himself with the ultimate rebel?

The Satanism of popular mythology was largely invented by gothic horror authors to thrill their readers. The Satanist was a scarcely human, hooded creature who committed acts of unspeakable evil with no obvious motive beyond wickedness for its own sake.

THE DEVIL'S DOCTRINES

Anton LaVey at home in the rare 1968 documentary about the Church of Satan entitled Satanis.

The pithiest version of the Church of Satan's central doctrines are 'The Nine Satanic Statements', first published in Anton LaVey's *Satanic Bible*. They are: 1. Satan represents indulgence instead of abstinence. 2. Satan represents vital existence instead of spiritual pipe dreams. 3. Satan represents undefiled wisdom, instead of hypocritical self-deceit. 4. Satan represents kindness to those who deserve it instead of love wasted on ingrates. 5. Satan represents vengeance instead of turning the other cheek. 6. Satan represents responsibility to the responsible instead of concern for psychic vampires. 7. Satan represents man as just another animal – sometimes better, more often worse than those who walk on all fours – who, because of his "divine spiritual and intellectual development" has become the most vicious animal of all. 8. Satan represents all of the so-called sins, as they all lead to physical, mental, or emotional gratification. 9. Satan has been the best friend the Church has ever had, as he has kept it in business all these years.

Much of this has echoed in Marilyn Manson's own pronouncements. On a talk show, he declared, 'There's an old saying that the Devil has always been the church's best friend, because he's kept them in business. And I think . . . they picked me to be that . . . I don't mind the protesting, I just wish that they would get the facts straight, because they think that I do a lot of things, but I am really about individuality.' The 'old saying' was, in fact, LaVey's ninth Satanic statement, but one of the many fundamentalist Christian misconceptions about the Antichrist Superstar was that he 'preached' from *The Satanic Bible* onstage, or had Church of Satan 'tracts' distributed to the audience. As neither an organised religion nor an evangelical recruiting drive, the Church of Satan is a radical non-conformist movement communicating solely through ideas – some of them expressed, subtly and otherwise, through the music and performance of Marilyn Manson.

In the cold light of day, he made little or no sense outside the fevered confines of horror fiction.

In the 1980s, however, fundamentalist Christians in the USA and across the world began to claim society was infiltrated by a conspiracy of 'satanic child abusers'. Their charges were based entirely on fanaticism and fantasy, but, with influential allies in media and government, they almost managed to convince a gullible world to usher in a new age of witch-hunts.

By the time Marilyn Manson came on the scene in the 1990s, a combination of common sense and investigative journalism had effectively ended the hysteria – but its influence can still be felt in the witch-burning motifs in the song 'Dogma', and references to child abuse on *Smells Like Children*. Another interesting side-effect of the satanic panic was that it ironically inspired a number of young self-styled 'Satanists', who had no more authentic sources on which to base their lifestyles.

Most of the petty crimes and suburban tragedies the fundamentalists highlighted as evidence of their conspiracy were actually influenced by their own propaganda, blended with elements of cheap novels and horror movies. It's a truly satanic concept – the ignorant bringing their own anxieties into concrete existence, conjuring up their own devils with the power of morbid fear. Pious bigots ranting against imaginary devils had created a generation of young malcontents eager to sign infernal pacts.

There are few better examples of this than Marilyn Manson. The young Brian Warner eagerly embraced the 'Satanism' he was warned of by his teachers at the Christian Heritage School. Their lists of forbidden 'satanic' records were menus of musical recommendation. Nightmares of the imminent apocalypse they predicted turned into curious dreams, filled with anticipation rather than fear. As he would later recall, warnings that the Devil was always watching him both frightened and titillated the boy. Most significantly, the Antichrist – portrayed as the ultimate villain by his teachers – became a deviant role model for Brian Warner. 'I am something that America has created out of its own fear,' he later observed, when his transformation into the ultimate anti-hero was complete.

Just as Christian fables played their role in formulating Marilyn Manson, so did the crude fictional portrayals of Satanism in sensationalist comic-books and movies. This was pop-culture Satanism – while the fictional breed were typically powerful, frightening figures, the kids they inspired were largely motivated by powerlessness and frustration. These teenage rebels – described as 'dabblers' and portrayed as outer initiates of the 'Satanic conspiracy' by evangelical Christians – were regarded with amused disdain by most authentic Satanists.

The 'Teen Dabbler' chapter in Marilyn's autobiography (see 'Drugs and Disease' – Chapter Four) describes Brian Warner's first encounter with Satanism in its most facile, adolescent form. He retrospectively dramatises the whole scene, comparing the dabbler who 'initiates' him (an older boy named Crowell) to 'Richard Ramirez the Night Stalker'. (Ramirez could be described as the ultimate dabbler gone wrong, a young man

THE DEVIL MADE ME DO IT

Most alleged 'satanic crimes' consisted of adolescents from dysfunctional backgrounds crudely murdering a family member or fellow student, usually under the influence of drugs or alcohol. The discovery of an Iron Maiden album or copy of *The Satanic Bible* at the troubled teen's house was sufficient for religiously-motivated cops, influenced by spurious seminars on 'cult crime', to label the case 'satanic'.

'That doesn't make it a "ritual murder,"' observed Anton LaVey in Blanche Barton's history of the Church of Satan. 'It just makes juicy copy. I'd like to see the day when headlines read "Slasher reported to be involved in Christian group" with the accompanying article outlining the incriminating evidence found in the killer's apartment – pictures of saints on the walls, the *Holy Bible* and other Christian books found on shelves, various crosses in small jewellery boxes. With these supposed Satanic crimes, "evidence of Satanic involvement" doesn't have anything to do with the crime itself – might not have anything to do with Satanism! – but is picked out because it piques people's prurient interests.'

Christians have also highlighted various murderers as members of mythical satanic sects – if the criminals themselves co-operate, it's because they enjoy the notoriety or hope to get early parole by 'confessing' and becoming born-again Christians. In every case, evidence of these criminal 'cults' is conspicuous by its absence, and many authorities have dismissed their confessions as fairy tales. Three of the best known criminals have lent their names to Marilyn Manson band-members: Henry Lee Lucas (who we have already met), David Berkowitz (the Son of Sam) and Richard Ramirez (the Night Stalker).

Berkowitz subjected New York to a thirteen-month long reign of terror beginning in July of 1976. By the time of his arrest the portly inadequate – who stalked lovers' lanes with a .44 revolver – had killed six people. He earned his bizarre nickname from letters sent to police and newspapers, wherein he announced himself as the 'Son of Sam'. In captivity, he grandiosely claimed to be part of a secret occult conspiracy, but cynics noted how he also said he'd been commanded to kill by his next-door neighbour's black Labrador.

Ramirez was a cat burglar with a penchant for the heavy metal band AC/DC and a sadistic streak a mile wide. During 1985 he killed, tortured and raped over a dozen victims while robbing their Los Angeles homes, leaving a spray-painted pentagram as his calling card. When apprehended the habitual drug abuser and kleptomaniac maintained his façade, making 'devil signs' and sinister comments to the press, but no-one ever seriously suggested he belonged to any cult or sect.

who took the media caricature of the Satanist to heart as a role model, and the pathological fantasy to its illogical extreme.)

Crowell's room is a shrine to 'black magic, heavy metal, self-mutilation and conspicuous drug consumption. Like my grandfather's basement, the room represented both my fears and desires.' The site of Crowell's Black Masses, in contrast to the gothic grandeur of the fictional satanic temple, is a squalid abandoned house full of obscene graffiti, abandoned drug paraphernalia and gay porn. Unlike those who would see the place as a den of metaphysical evil, or sneer at it as a shrine to dumb delinquency, the teenage Brian seems to be able to identify some authentic power, or even magic, hidden beneath its sordid veneer – as if its very existence, its grimly romantic aspirations in the face of adversity, was of significance. Ultimately, it would prove a catalyst that helped trigger his evolution from Wormboy to Antichrist Superstar.

It's often erroneously stated that in order to be a Satanist you must believe in God. This is true only in the case of 'devil-worshippers', who take the villains of biblical lore and turn them into their idols and prophets. As long ago as the second century, there were sects whose re-interpretations of the gospels led them to revere its villains – like the serpent who tempted Eve in the Garden of Eden, or Cain whose jealousy of the favours bestowed upon him by God finally overcame him resulting in the murder of his brother Abel. 'It's just that history was written by winners,' as Marilyn Manson has observed. 'In *The Bible*'s case, the winner is God.' (Or indeed, the Christian Church, who claim to be his spokesmen on earth.)

In the thirteenth century a cult was reported by authorities in Germany, known as the Luciferians, who revered Lucifer as a true god of wisdom and pleasure, traitorously cast into the darkness by the Christian God. As Marilyn has reflected, 'There's a lot of great stories and a lot of great values in *The Holy Bible*, and I actually relate to a lot of them. The character, the idea, or the part of my personality that I describe as *Antichrist Superstar*, is a lot like Lucifer in *The Bible*. Someone who was kicked out of heaven because he wanted to be God.'

Aleister Crowley, one of Marilyn Manson's most profound influences, rejected the title of devil-worshipper or Satanist (though he privately confessed to being a black magician). This is a reflection of the Great Beast's ego – he didn't want to be limited to that one role, and evidently considered himself, as would Marilyn, 50 years later, 'bigger than Satan'. In reality, however, the Beast's creed was largely inspired by a radical reinterpretation of the biblical Book of Revelations, turning its demonic entities into his heroes – devil-worship, by any other name.

Today, 'devil-worshippers' are only marginally more significant than the teenage 'dabblers' who play at Satanism. The Temple of Set – who venerate the Egyptian god Set, who they regard as an earlier form of the Christian Devil – were formed in the 1970s by defectors from the Church of Satan. They wanted a *real* devil to worship, while Anton

LaVey preached that Satan was actually a complex, purely symbolic figure. Blending elements of LaVeyan Satanism with a heavy dash of Crowley, the Temple of Set's membership are nonetheless moving to ditch the terms 'Satanism' or 'devil-worship' as unnecessarily provocative.

True Satanism is an anti-religion based not on faith, but doubt, and is a specifically modern phenomenon. The first use of the word in English can be traced back to a sixteenth-century bishop of London, exiled at the time, to describe his enemies back in England. Significantly, these people were not devil-worshippers but militant atheists who showed their contempt for the Church with profane language and godless lifestyles. As per today, Satanists never worshipped anything or anyone but themselves. Setting themselves against Christ, and all reputed messiahs, they are truly – as Marilyn Manson observes – anti-Christs.

Perhaps the most significant work in the Satanic literary tradition is the epic seventeenth-century poem *Paradise Lost*, by the blind English puritan John Milton. Contrary to the pious intentions of its author, *Paradise Lost* creates a noble Devil in revolt against divine tyranny – famously declaring it is 'Better to reign in hell, than serve in heaven', the motto of all romantic rebels. The poem not only sowed the seeds for a sympathetic Satan, but, in translating *The Bible*'s central story into a popular poem, demonstrated that the Christian holy book is a collection of ancient fictional tales rather than the divine word of God Himself.

Marilyn Manson describes Satanism as 'simply part of what I believe in, along with Dr Seuss, Dr Hook, Nietzsche, and *The Bible*, which I also believe in. I just have my own interpretation.' Like many Satanists, however, he also encountered Milton's Satan at an early age, particularly struck by the Devil's role in the genesis of mankind as described in *Paradise Lost*. Marilyn interprets God's creation of humanity in the poem as a direct response to Satan's rebellion, inspired by the Almighty's need to bully or manipulate his creations. This, in Manson's eyes, implies that humankind has its mythic origin not only in divine creation but also infernal rebellion. Anton LaVey founded the first public satanic institution, the Church of Satan, in San Francisco, 1966. Attempting to define the satanic tradition, he pulled together a diverse collection of infernal thinkers and artists from over the centuries, weaving them into a coherent anti-religion. Among those LaVey considered tacit Satanists were the carnal holyman Rasputin, cynical journalist Ambrose Bierce and carnival showman P. T. Barnum. Perhaps the most important figure in LaVey's canon of satanic saints, however, was Friedrich Nietzsche who declared (as Marilyn Manson later did), 'I am the Antichrist.'

The Black Pope is not alone in regarding the German philosopher as an inherent Satanist. In his book *Masks of Satan*, Catholic historian Christopher Nugent observes, 'Nietzsche knew what he was about when he rechristened himself the Antichrist. Nietzsche had chosen his own weapons, and when we behold the man against the

The Anti-Christ as envisaged in La vie de l' Antechrist, *printed at Lyons in the late fifteenth century.*

The Antichrist is a complex theological figure. He appears most famously in the book of Revelations, the apocalyptic final book of *The Bible*, though he is also alluded to in other biblical texts such as the Book of 'Thessalonians' where he is described as 'a man of sin' and 'a son of perdition'. There is some confusion as to whether the Antichrist is a specific individual, or simply someone who's against Christ. Most scholars now believe it was a general insult aimed at heretics and unbelievers (this is the interpretation favoured by Marilyn Manson), but over time the Antichrist changed into a mythic servant of the Devil whose arrival signalled the end of the world.

This myth was very popular by the Middle Ages, and a large number of books were written concerning the Antichrist's imminent arrival and his incarnation in specific historical figures. Over the years the Roman Emperor Nero, the French military dictator Napoleon Bonaparte and the leader of the German Third Reich, Adolf Hitler, have all been identified as the Antichrist. Recent years have seen a revival in the myth's popularity, principally because of successful Hollywood treatments like *Rosemary's Baby* (1968) and *The Omen* (1976), which adapted fundamentalist conspiracy fantasies into horror stories. Marilyn Manson recalls watching *The Omen* as a child when nightmares about the Apocalypse, inspired by his Christian teachers, began to haunt him. The film concerns a child called Damien, unwittingly adopted into a powerful American political family, who is really the son of the Devil. 'Remember . . .' ran the ads, 'you have been warned.'

background we are prompted to conclude that he was a seminal satanist, that his superman and satanist were essentially one, and that this is a satanism for which Nietzsche was willing to sacrifice everything – consequently, worth taking seriously.' Marilyn Manson would agree, once describing Satanism as being 'about realising, much like Nietzsche said, that you are your own god'.

Over the years, the Black Pope ushered a number of celebrities through the doors of the Black House, the San Francisco Vatican of his anti-religion. At its foundation, the Church of Satan played host to many of the writers associated with the legendary *Weird Tales* horror magazine that launched the career of H. P. Lovecraft. (LaVey considered the eerie fictions of *Weird Tales* to be more truly satanic than the 'authentic' spell books that inspired more traditional occultists.) Later, song-and-dance-man Sammy Davis, Junior was attracted to the Church of Satan by the black-Jewish racial origins that made him a natural outsider in Hollywood. Actress Jayne Mansfield, the brassy blonde often dismissed as a poor man's Marilyn Monroe, found her lustful nature celebrated in LaVey's temple to carnality.

By the early 1980s the Church of Satan had melted back into the shadows, its founder a misanthropic recluse. (There are parallels here between the Black Pope's self-imposed exile, seeking company only among the mannequins in his 'Den of Iniquity', and Marilyn's decision in late 1999 to escape 'civilisation' and retreat into the virtual reality of cyberspace.) LaVey's enemies started rumours that the Church of Satan was defunct, or bankrupt, with rival groups such as the Temple of Set portraying themselves as its successor, while some even whispered that the Black Pope was dead. Nevertheless, a few counterculture cognoscenti continued to seek out the legendary Satanist – perhaps most significantly, the controversial industrial musician Boyd Rice who helped re-energise the Church and its founder in the 1980s. He was the first of a new generation of offbeat entertainers and cult figures to be initiated into the Church of Satan. Later initiates would include King Diamond, vocalist with Scandinavian black metal pioneers Mercyful Fate, and cult cabaret singer Marc Almond.

By the 1990s the Church of Satan was ready for action again, as a new electricity began to run through the organisation and its founder. LaVey began recruiting a new hierarchy of priests and magisters to spread his unholy doctrine by word and example, while the grotto system of contact points across the USA and Europe, idle for a decade, was now revived. Among those newly associated with the Church of Satan was, of course, Marilyn Manson, ordained as a Reverend by the Black Pope in October 1994.

With the shock-rocker's fortunes on the rise, he undoubtedly helped raise the Church Of Satan's profile. Blanche Barton – Church of Satan administrator, LaVey's secretary, and the mother of his son, Xerxes – observed, 'We've received a number of enquiries from kids who first got interested in Satanism because of Marilyn Manson's music and attitudes. The Doctor [LaVey] feels one reason Mr Manson's popular is because he's the Real Thing. He makes no secret about his advocacy of true Satanic ideals – and

he's articulate enough to explain exactly what those ideals are, rather than just the typical spook stories of sacrifices and criminal cartels.' There was talk of Barton, who was responsible for LaVey's biography *The Secret Life of a Satanist*, writing the Reverend Manson's life story – though this never ultimately came to pass. So, while the Church of Satan was enjoying a raised profile, and improved sales of LaVey's *Satanic Bible*, what did their most famous new recruit get from his association with the church and its founder?

'LaVey is a huge influence on a lot of the things I do,' Marilyn has explained. 'I'm not part of any specific religion but that's [the Church of Satan is] not a religion anyway, if you're really into it.' The Black Pope's creed is a cabal of like-minded individuals rather than a cult, the relationship he cultivated with his congregation not one of shepherd and flock. 'I admired and respected him,' acclaimed Manson. 'We had a lot of things in common: We had experience as extravagant showmen, successfully placed curses on people, studied criminology and serial killers, found a kindred spirit in the writings of Nietzsche, and constructed a philosophy against repression and in support of nonconformity.'

In an interview in the Church of Satan's organ, *The Black Flame*, published just prior to the release of *Antichrist Superstar*, the newly-ordained Reverend was asked whether Satanism had influenced his music. 'Not overtly – subconsciously,' came the response. 'I have to thank LaVey for inspiration. I incorporate Satanic philosophy, at some times more subtly than others. It gets across the philosophy without the name "Satanism". After people get close to me, I let them know of my affiliation with the Church. The band isn't overt with the symbolism of Satanism, no upside-down crosses or baphomets. I have been more outspoken about Satanism in the last year or so, and the fans seem to understand the philosophy . . . The concert is Satanic. Just by being in the audience, you are entering my own personal Satanic ritual. However, I'm not a salesman for the Church of Satan. I get adrenal energy from the crowd, and they get it from me. This energy motivates me, makes me feel completely vital on stage. After the show, I feel drained and have no more emotion, which is the exact prescription for a ritual in *The Satanic Bible*. I find performing to be the most powerful thing I've tapped into.'

The idea of creativity – especially music – being somehow linked with the Devil is an old one. Throughout the Church of Satan's history, increasing emphasis had been placed on entertainment and the media as vehicles for 'black magic', as opposed to the traditional activities of the sorcerer waving his wand at thin air in a darkened room. Even in the early days, when melodramatic rituals were still a regular occurrence at the Black House, LaVey emphasised them as 'psychodrama'. An increasing number of Church of Satan members were professional writers, artists and musicians who recognised that the true 'black arts' involved manipulating the world around you with your creative skills. As time passed the Black Pope himself, an accomplished keyboard player, concentrated more of his energies into music as a vehicle for magical transformation.

Asked what it was like to meet LaVey, the Reverend Manson responded that it was

'Flattering, exciting – an interesting person to meet, inspirational-wise. I've had a lot of great conversations with him. I have listened to him play music at his house. I felt like a part of his family, as if he were a father figure to me. People have often asked me "What is Satanic music? Is it just what Dr LaVey plays?" Yes it is, and no it isn't. If you grew up listening to the music of the forties, that music would be evocative to you. In my case, it was the music of the seventies and the eighties. People my age find this music much more powerful. Satanic music is music that affects your life. I had musical influences from Black Sabbath and other groups like Alice Cooper, David Bowie, the Stooges, and KISS. It wasn't necessarily the music I liked, but that they stood out as icons.'

This is associated with a LaVeyan doctrine, that the forgotten popular tunes of your childhood have latent magical powers, a doctrine reflected in the music of many performers with Church of Satan connections. 'I think there's different elements of what people call magic in music,' explains Marilyn, 'some artists know how to interpret it, some don't. I think your success gauges how well you use magic. And I think that magic is as simple as your ability to entertain people, your ability to allure people with what you do.'

LaVey had a background in the carnivals and travelling fairs that criss-crossed the US in the 1930s and 1940s. He expressed much of his doctrine using the imagery and terminology of the carnivals, the same kind of language echoed by Marilyn Manson in describing his most satanic album, *Antichrist Superstar*: 'It's like an amusement park. It's part of people's nature to be attracted to their own death and to fear. That's why this record is three cycles of death happening, and that's why people will gravitate toward it – whether in outrage or with open arms, people will gravitate to it.'

More darkly, LaVey's misanthropy, which fuelled much of his creed, can also be detected in many of the Reverend Manson's pronouncements, particularly those reflecting his darker moods: 'My contempt for the rest of humanity is the driving force behind my creativity. The fact that other people completely lack the motivation to live, their lack of creativity and their ignorance, those are my main driving forces.'

Marilyn also shares LaVey's conviction that the chief enemy of the modern Satanist is not just the Christian Church but also the subtle conformity imposed by corporate America, most powerfully through the medium of television. 'Christianity is really responsible for consumerism,' he opines. 'The idea of blind faith has really ruined America in some ways, because there's this underlying theme of fascism that nobody's willing to accept. We're being controlled by our own stupidity and weaknesses. You turn on the TV, and if you don't buy this type of shampoo, you're not going to get laid, or if you don't buy this car, your friends aren't gonna accept you, and all of your friends are making fun of you behind your back because you have acne. It just eats away at your soul. It makes you so dependent that you're scared to make your own decisions.'

Marilyn plays with the concept of fascism – suggesting comparisons with those more subtle compulsions to conform that are the province of the Church and consumer society. Such herd mentality is in direct contradiction of the merciless Social Darwinist individualism advocated by LaVey, and endorsed by Marilyn Manson – which, in turn, is also labelled 'fascist' by some of its opponents.

GOD IS A NUMBER YOU CANNOT COUNT TO

***Antichrist Superstar* is the most overtly satanic of Marilyn Manson's releases. Both lyrically and graphically, the album is a blend of sinister symbolism and occult imagery. His passion for puzzles, word games and conundrums is well known, and on this album Marilyn indulges it via traditional magical sources. When talking about the recording sessions, its creator makes particular reference to the Kabbala and numerology. Both are common occult disciplines, utilised by magicians such as Aleister Crowley. Put crudely, numerology is occultic mathematics – a system that assumes the hidden truths of the universe are concealed within numbers.**

The Kabbala is a mystical system with roots in medieval Judaism, still studied by some Jewish scholars. To understand God and Creation, and the connections between the two, it employs a language of symbols that either depicts a journey through a series of 'spheres', or shows creation and the path to divinity as branches on a tree. Many occult systems, like numerology and the tarot, have their basis in Kabbalism.

The greatest influence Anton LaVey has had on Marilyn Manson was in the encouragement of personal evolution. As he says in *The Long Hard Road Out of Hell*, 'The most valuable thing he did that day [of his first meeting with LaVey] was to help me understand and come to terms with the deadness, hardness and apathy I was feeling about myself and the world around me, explaining that it was all necessary, a middle step in an evolution from an innocent child to an intelligent, powerful being capable of making a mark on the world.'

The stress and excess of the band's early days were taking their toll. He recalls in his autobiography how his essential humanity was gradually dwindling away. A car wreck happens in front of him, and one of the victims reaches out to Manson to hold her as she dies, but, increasingly desensitised, he just walks on by. Perhaps most outrageously, he had even been contemplating murder: 'At the time, taking someone's life seemed like a necessary growing and learning experience, like losing your virginity or having a child.'

Marilyn's response to this increasing numbness and moral confusion was to deliberately immerse himself in a process of self-destruction, to bring about an internal apocalypse. This process became part of the recording of *Antichrist Superstar*, as its creator testified at the time. 'We experimented in pain, experimented in narcotics, Hebrew Kabbalism, numerology has become very important on the new album – when you look at it very carefully people can read a lot into the numbers and symbols.' Using ritualised drugs and degradation, Marilyn Manson shed Brian Warner's skin to become the Antichrist, 'the Angel with the Scabbed Wings', 'The Man that you Fear'.

'The album,' he acclaimed of *Antichrist Superstar*, 'is really a soundtrack to our lives. I look at this record as a living piece of art that continues to grow as people continue to buy it. We haven't come to the conclusion yet. It's a bit of prophecy of what will come. If you believe in something strong enough, you can make it happen. In the Kabbala, there's this idea that the world can only be ended by mankind inviting destruction upon itself. Everyone's fear of Marilyn Manson is really what has created it. So, this record is a ritual to bring that about, and each time someone plays it, it takes them one step closer to the apocalypse. Whether that's in your mind or not is as easy as people finally killing off God in their minds and becoming themselves, believing in themselves.'

This internal apocalypse has parallels in many traditions. The process of putting yourself through hell to achieve a transformation presents itself in many guises – for example, in the politics and culture of a nation moving from nihilism to fascism, or decadence; or in the Decadent artistic tradition, where a poet subjects himself to utter degradation and misery in order to truly understand beauty. Walter Pater expressed it well in his 1873 essay *The Renaissance*, which became a bible for English Decadents – 'the way to perfection is through a series of disgusts'. As Brian Stableford observes in *Moral Ruins*, 'The quest for new sensations – which, inevitably, can also be seen as a search for new sins – is sometimes seen even by the Decadents themselves as little more than an elaborate process of self-destructiveness.' There are few more vivid examples of this than Arthur Rimbaud's nightmarish prose poem '*Une Saison en enfer*' ('*A Season in Hell*') which describes his redemptive journey to the very depths of depravity.

As with Marilyn Manson, Rimbaud's inner journey is fuelled partially by drugs. As Aldous Huxley observes, the drug-induced spiritual experience need not be a pleasant one, but may be just as valid if it is nightmarish: 'Where, for any reason, physical or moral, the psychological dispositions are unsatisfactory, the removal of obstacles by a drug or by ascetic practices will result in a negative rather than a positive spiritual experience. Such an infernal experience is extremely distressing, but may also be extremely salutary. There are plenty of people to whom a few hours in hell – the hell that they themselves have done so much to create – could do a world of good.'

Aleister Crowley also talks about crossing an abyss, a hellish vacuum, to evolve into a new form. On a personal level, this took place when he conducted a series of magical rites in the lonely mountains of North Africa to invoke Chronozon, 'the mighty devil of the Abyss', whilst being ritually buggered by his assistant, the poet Victor Neuburg.

Crowley believed that he was successful in inviting Chronozon to possess him, then conquering the demon and evolving to a higher state of being. On a historical level, he preached that the new aeon of 'Do what thou wilt' could not be realised until the world was washed by a sea of blood and chaos. The abyss is central to the philosophy of Friedrich Nietzsche, who describes the evolutionary path to the übermensch as a process of 'self-overcoming', a struggle to cross the hellish abyss of nihilism within ourselves. 'Only in the savage forest of vice can new domains of knowledge be found,' wrote the German philosopher.

Orthodox Christianity, as is well known, regards spiritual evolution as very often attainable only via a hellish rite of passage. The early Church Fathers wandered into the inhospitable deserts to live as hermits, in the hope that their monstrous discomfort would somehow purify and enlighten them. Indeed, Christ's time on the cross could serve no purpose in the divine plan unless his torture was of some spiritual significance, suggesting that even Jesus had to cross the abyss in order to redeem humanity. The idea persists today in diluted form, familiar in the modern exercise cult where people are instructed to 'go for the burn' in search of the ultimate 'exercise high'. 'Working out' may develop a more muscular body mass, but only after the muscles have been, initially, painfully broken down (this idea – achieving health through willpower – also echoes Nietzschean doctrine).

Anton LaVey died in 1997. Marilyn Manson's album *Mechanical Animals*, released in the following year, seemed almost devoid of Satanic content in contrast to *Antichrist Superstar*. Was the Reverend Manson spurning the influence of his Black Pope, who he once described as a 'father figure'? While portraying *Mechanical Animals* as a direct sequel to *Antichrist Superstar*, their eponymous lead singer was eager to make it clear that, as far as he was concerned, Marilyn Manson had made their statement on religion. Even so, elements of LaVeyan Satanism remained.

'"Mechanical animals" is the way I describe mankind and the path it's following. That people look and act like human beings, but inside, we're losing our souls, that we numb ourselves with drugs, we numb ourselves with television. We numb ourselves with the Internet, with prescription drugs, with whatever we can find, because everyone's afraid to be an individual. And *Mechanical Animals* is the fear that I have for the world . . . The idea of *Mechanical Animals* is that man makes himself more and more irrelevant with what he creates. You kind of have to remember where it all comes from. If machines someday replace men, they would realise that you can't replace the human soul, so they'd have to try to start manufacturing humans again.'

But while Marilyn expressed his fear for the future, a world where people were so insensitive as to be indistinguishable from the machines around them, by way of direct contrast LaVey had relished the prospect of artificial people. Indeed, he listed its promotion in his 1988 'Five Point Pentagonal Revisionism Program' as one of the Church of Satan's goals. Artificial human companions would allow satisfying sex for the masses without contributing further to overpopulation, and facilitate 'politically correct slavery'. Marilyn Manson's *Mechanical Animals* had more in common with the metaphorical 'Mechanical Man' – who Charlie Manson mocked in song for losing touch with his true nature – than the literal mechanical animals LaVey wished to construct for his own pleasure. Most of all, the Black Pope – who preached that people were not reminded of their own inadequacies often enough – believed that the production of androids would highlight just how expendable and interchangeable most people were.

Even Marilyn Manson – Reverend of the Church of Satan and a self-declared misanthrope – found this difficult to swallow, preferring to think of a redemptive finale to his *Mechanical Animals* fable. Marilyn and LaVey were agreed on the stupidity of most people (stupidity being the greatest Satanic sin), but, while Marilyn Manson talked about making people more intelligent, the Black Pope didn't believe this was possible and just growled darkly about finding a way of dealing with the stupid. How long a close association could have continued between two such powerful, egotistical personalities is difficult to say, particularly in light of Marilyn's penchant for re-inventing himself.

In an interview with *Creem* in the winter of 1998, Marilyn was asked about his Church of Satan membership card. He responded casually, 'I don't think I have that anymore. I lost it.' It was a relationship always destined to be problematic. As much as the Church of Satan approved of Marilyn's manic individualism, and flair for theatre, there was some disquiet over his flamboyant drug use, androgyny and self-destructive tendencies. Both they and he were unhappy with baseless suggestions that he was being groomed as the new Black Pope, and it was something of a relief to all concerned when Marilyn Manson, with characteristic pomp, took to declaring himself 'bigger than Satan'.

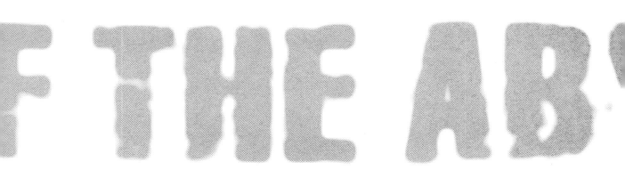

Chapter Nine

MARTYRED MONSTERS

The success of *Antichrist Superstar*, Marilyn Manson's breakthrough album, posed an interesting artistic challenge: how do you top the Apocalypse?

The Long Hard Road Out of Hell, which can be read as a companion to *Antichrist Superstar*, provides an answer in the penultimate chapter, which concludes with the words 'I was even bigger than Satan.' It was a soundbite repeated in a number of interviews throughout 1998.

Was Marilyn Manson indeed bigger than Satan? Bigger than the infernal entity who inspired Niccolò Paganini, the greatest violinist of the nineteenth century? Bigger than the tormented anti-hero who served as a role model for the most brilliant of the English Romantic poets? Bigger than the mysterious stranger who, down at the crossroads, tuned the guitar of Robert Johnson, the Delta bluesman whose style gave birth to rock'n'roll?

The footnotes of rock history are littered with bands who, after recording an album with a demonic theme, turned their attentions to less contentious subjects. Some got away with it, cashing in on Satanism's powerful iconography to record a breakthrough album, then distancing themselves from the subject to avoid negative feedback (Black Sabbath, Iron Maiden and Motley Crüe are obvious examples). But many more went under. Anton LaVey warned that those who use the Devil to obtain power or success (and in Satanism, the creative arts are synonymous with the black arts) and then deny him will lose all they have gained. Perhaps the long list of performers who went bust after first exploiting the Devil is LaVey's law in action.

Mechanical Animals, the 1998 follow-up to *Antichrist Superstar*, was much better received by the press than its predecessor. However, the fan reaction was less universally positive. The music sounded less abrasive and more 'commercial', the image seemed less confrontational, the concept less powerful – some Spooky Kids interpreted it as a betrayal, rather than a progression. However, while sales were not as phenomenal as those of *Antichrist Superstar*, Marilyn Manson, as a band, had successfully navigated a difficult stage in their development.

While not universally popular with his fans, Marilyn's decision to ditch the Antichrist Superstar persona in favour of the decadent Omega character was well-timed, particularly in the light of the oncoming Columbine controversy. Defending himself against charges of promoting violence was, relatively, easier in his *Mechanical Animals* phase than it would have been in his previous predatory incarnation. As he expressed the contrast between the two personas: '*Antichrist Superstar* was a lot of parallels between my life and someone like Lucifer. *Mechanical Animals* has a lot more parallels between me and Jesus Christ.'

The transformation from satanic villain to messianic character was radical by anybody's standards, though it was the martyrdom of Jesus that obviously appealed to Marilyn. Martyrdom is the dark, unspoken side of rock celebrity – many rock biographies are catalogues of personal disasters and early deaths, of earthly messiahs crucified by their own self-indulgence. Many fans secretly like to see their idols meet untimely ends, thrilled by the romantic tragedy of glamorous talent cut down in its prime.

And so rumours of a spectacular onstage suicide by Marilyn Manson started to circulate. He himself dates the start of these rumours to Halloween 1996, noting in his journal, 'I've died so much in the past year, I don't think there's much to kill.' Similar rumours had circulated two decades before concerning Iggy Pop, the original rock'n'roll maverick with a penchant for public self-mutilation (though, in Iggy's case, he was then an obscure cult figure living dangerously on the edges of the music scene, who could have died at any time). But, so the reasoning went, if Marilyn was willing to cut his chest on stage, why not his wrists? The Dead to the World tour was reaching a level of intensity where it appeared to need some kind of climax – what could be more spectacular than the public suicide of its main protagonist? As he would observe of his fans the following year, 'No matter how much they love you, they want a tragedy.' (Or, as the final lines of David Bowie's 'Ziggy Stardust' have it: 'Like a leper messiah / When the kids had killed the man I had to break up the band.')

Evangelical Christians have long tried to construct connections between Satanism, rock music and suicide, accusations they have tried to prove in court. (Both efforts – against metal bands Judas Priest and Ozzy Osbourne's Blizzard of Oz – were dismal failures.) Satanists reverse this accusation, calling Christianity a death cult: Satanism's lack of belief in an afterlife gives value and urgency to *this* life, while Christianity's fixation with self-sacrifice and martyrdom is one big death wish. While the Satanist's attitude to martyrdom is one of contempt, this growing element in Marilyn Manson's personal obsessions may have reflected his growing distance from the Church of Satan.

The demonic perspective is best expressed in the play *The Devil's Disciple* by George Bernard Shaw (who Anton LaVey regarded as implicitly a Satanist), in which martyrdom

YOU SAY YOU WANT A REVOLUTION?

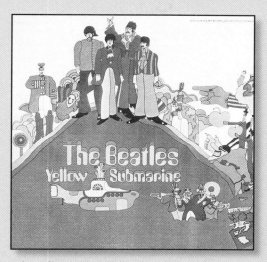

The Yellow Submarine - *harmless psychedelia - but Christians claim John Lennon is making the sign of the devil's horns!...*

It seems odd to associate the Beatles, standard bearers for the love generation, with Marilyn Manson. Surely the Rolling Stones, with the demonic overtones of their late-1960s material, would be more appropriate? Or Elvis Presley – whose success turned him into a bloated caricature, and who thus, like Marilyn, symbolises a bizarre side of Americana? But early Marilyn Manson material features songs with punned titles based on Beatles numbers like 'Revelation #9' (taken from 'Revolution #9'), and 'Lucy in the Sky with Demons' ('Lucy in the Sky with Diamonds'), while Marilyn credits the Beatles' 1968 *White Album* as an influence on *Mechanical Animals*. Perhaps no ambitious rock band can reach their peak without at least acknowledging the Beatles, who pretty much invented modern pop music.

The Beatles also had a darker side that contrasts with their modern image as chirpy, peace-loving moptops, centring on John Lennon, the group's most talented but volatile member. Beneath his well-publicised persona as a campaigner for peace and understanding, Lennon could be cynical, selfish and loutish. His curiously surreal short stories and poems also seemed to revel in cruelty and misery.

The most sinister aspect of the Beatles, however, can hardly be blamed on any member of the band. The Manson Family were big fans of *The White Album*, claiming that Charlie himself heard prophecies in its lyrics of an apocalyptic race war called 'Helter Skelter' (the title of a song later covered by Marilyn Manson), and that other messages prompted him to order the murders that were to provoke this war. Many (including Charlie himself) have denied this, but the chilling graffiti written in a victim's blood at one of the murder scenes included the legend 'Healter Skelter' (sic).

is described as 'the only way in which a man can become famous without ability'. However, Marilyn Manson revelled in the irony of his Christian opponents' malevolence on the Dead to the World tour, expressing their dedication to a creed of universal love by threatening him with violence. 'I'm sure Ozzy [Osbourne] had his problems in the past, but I don't think he ever had as many death threats as we did,' he reflected. 'Hundreds of them. Usually threatening to blow the building up.'

He was acutely aware that his martyrdom might become more than symbolic, that some heavily-armed Christian extremist might decide to assassinate 'the Antichrist'. Such things have happened before. Marilyn's 'bigger than Satan' quote was a deliberate, ironic echo of the notorious suggestion made by John Lennon before a 1966 US tour that the Beatles were 'bigger than Jesus'. Pious Americans had long been suspicious of the British rock group, but Lennon's blasphemous comment was a declaration of war. The tour was plagued by a storm of public protests that reached an intensity seldom matched until the Dead to the World tour 30 years later. Christian antipathy towards the Beatles reached its grim climax in 1980, when Lennon, the most outspoken ex-member, was shot outside his apartment in New York. His assassin was a young man named Mark Chapman, who had just become a born-again Christian.

Bizarrely, Chapman had been an obsessive Beatles fan. However, since 1966 his hero Lennon had been cultivating a Christ-like image, consciously or otherwise, complete with long hair, beard and flamboyant statements in favour of world peace. There was even talk of him taking the title role in the 1972 rock musical *Jesus Christ Superstar* (he turned it down when producers refused to consider Yoko Ono as the Virgin Mary).

Whether Lennon's Christ affectations were a subtle act of blasphemy, or whether he genuinely saw himself in a messianic light, perhaps it's not so surprising that an unstable fan might be pushed over the edge when told that his idol is a false messiah, an Antichrist. Lennon had predicted his own violent death, dreaming about it regularly, and telling friends that death by the bullet was a 'modern day crucifixion'.

'Christianity has given us an image of death and sexuality that we have based our culture around,' Marilyn Manson has noted. 'A half-naked dead man hangs in most homes and around our necks, and we have just taken that for granted all our lives. Is it a symbol of hope or hopelessness? The world's most famous murder-suicide was also the birth of a death icon — the blueprint for celebrity.'

The Antichrist Superstar seems to have been tempted by the charismatic appeal of the messianic role, to become 'bigger than Jesus'. He recalls how, at the first ever Marilyn Manson gig, he had recently had a mole removed, noting how it bled onto the Marilyn Monroe T-shirt he was wearing, giving her one red eye. He also notes that the 'wound' was in his side in the same location Christ's side was pierced by a Roman lance, according to biblical lore. In late 1996 he observed to an interviewer, 'Sometimes I think the most shocking thing I could do would be to behave politely and speak of Christian morality.'

In 1997, Reverend Manson of the Church of Satan announced to his Spooky-Kid

THE IMPORTANCE OF BEING OSCAR

Marilyn Manson has often referred to the important influence of the Irishman born as Oscar Fingal Flaherty O'Wills Wilde, in 1854. Upon moving to England, Wilde soon became as well-known for his theatrical dress and manners as for his writing. Today he is best remembered for his dry wit, no anthology of quotes complete without a few of his droll, acidic put-downs or cynically camp observations on life.

Wilde's love affair with London society came to an abrupt end when his private life became the subject of a high-profile court case in 1895. He was accused by the father of a close friend, a decadent aristocrat named Lord Alfred Douglas, of corrupting the young man. Furthermore, Douglas' father, the Marquess of Queensbury, accused Wilde of being a 'sodomite'. His bisexuality, for long the subject of gossip, now became a source of scandal. His conviction and subsequent imprisonment destroyed not only his reputation, but the sharp-but-brittle author's health.

Today he is viewed as a great literary character, martyred by Victorian sexual hypocrisy. There was, however, an almost demonic side to Oscar Wilde. His only novel, *The Picture of Dorian Gray*, concerns a deal made between the title character and the immoral Lord Henry Wotton, whereby all the wages of sin and debauchery will be etched onto a portrait of Gray instead of upon its subject. Many have interpreted this deal as a classic medieval satanic pact in decadent dress. More decadent still was Wilde's retelling of the biblical story of Salome, who seduces her stepfather King Herodias in order that he will behead John the Baptist. The critic Christopher Nassaar has described the play as a Black Mass, the basis of a 'satanic religion' based upon the adoration of 'evil beauty' instead of Christian virtue.

fans on a radio show, 'A long time ago, there was a man as misunderstood as we are and they nailed him to a fucking cross!' On a discussion panel that year, he discussed Christ with Lakita Garth, Miss Black California (according to *Raygun* magazine, 'a rabidly-judgemental embarrassment to Christian activism'). 'When we were talking about Christ and me being not like Christ,' recalled Marilyn, 'I mean, if you look at things from a different point of view, one person could see Christ as being someone a lot like me. Someone with long hair, had a lot of fans, a lot of people that followed. He had twelve disciples — that could have been his posse for all we know. He hung out with hookers. He drank. People were against him.'

For all this, Marilyn Manson was adamant: 'I don't want to be Christ.' In *The Long Hard Road Out of Hell,* however, he describes an interesting dream with messianic overtones. He dreams it is Judgement Day — the end of the world in Christian mythology

– and he is strapped to a huge cross parading on a float towards Times Square. Joyful crowds, anticipating their demise with joy, are pelting him with rotten fruit and vegetables.

While highlighting parallels between rock concerts and Hitler's Nuremberg rallies on the Dead to the World tour, Marilyn also struck an analogy with Jesus' Sermon on the Mount. 'Because what Christianity started out as wasn't anything more than what we saw at the show today. It was one person getting up and saying what he felt, and a lot of people going, "Yeah, I feel that too." Jesus was the first rock star, the first sex symbol and the first icon.'

By the time of *Mechanical Animals* Lucifer had all but disappeared from the imagery of the lyrics, and from interviews, replaced by Christ: 'It's not to say that what I'm presenting is Christian, but I'm finding comparisons between the alienation that occurred with Jesus as much as the alienation that occurs with me.' Marilyn even began to describe the progress from *Antichrist Superstar* to *Mechanical Animals* in messianic terms. 'Things need to go to a point of extremism in order to be born again, so we can once again appreciate the little things in life: sex, drugs and rock and roll. Things need to go past that point as far as they can go, and then we'll become innocent again. It's my job to sort of cleanse the world of all its sins. I'm offering myself up as a sacrifice to the world to become innocent again.'

This idea of immersing yourself in carnal excess in order to achieve redemption is nothing new. Some of the earliest heretical Christian sects – like the Carpocratians in the third century – were branded 'satanic' for their doctrines of salvation through sin. Some of the nineteenth-century Decadent writers believed you could only reach the heights of sanctity by experiencing the depths of depravity. T. S. Eliot, the celebrated poet, was a confirmed Christian who conceived the idea of 'redemptive Satanism'. Maintaining that immersion in sin had been a curious way to convert from Decadence to Christianity, he wrote, 'Satanism itself, so far as not merely an affectation, was an attempt to get into Christianity by the backdoor.'

The inspired but neurotic Decadent novelist J. K. Huysmans seems to have been a closet Catholic even when examining the darkest corners of the Parisian underworld. One of the themes of his satanic novel, *Là-Bas*, was the thin barrier between sainthood and Satanism, as illustrated by the relationship between medieval sodomite-sorcerer Gilles de Rais and his friend the virginal Saint Joan of Arc. The novel caused a minor scandal, one critic famously exclaiming that after such a book, Huysmans would have to choose between 'the muzzle of a pistol and the foot of the Cross'. Few were truly surprised when he opted for the latter and converted to Catholicism in 1892.

Many were surprised, however, at the conversion of Oscar Wilde while living in self-imposed exile in France. Wilde, the Irish-born decadent writer and celebrated wit, was convicted of sodomy in 1895 and sentenced to two years' hard labour. He emerged a broken man, dying in Paris in 1900. During the intervening years of exile, however,

THE CITY OF LOST ANGELS

For his third album, *Mechanical Animals*, Marilyn Manson returned for inspiration to the same city where he had recorded the first, *Portrait of an American Family* – which, with all its arch commentary on the connection between celebrity and serial murder, was recorded on the site of the notorious Manson-Tate murders. As his producer Trent Reznor observed at the time, 'The view from the front door is the best view of LA I've ever seen. It's amazing how beautiful looking down into a smog pit can be.'

Los Angeles is also home to Hollywood, the world-famous 'dream factory'. Its surrounding areas are also a polluted cultural melting pot, which has boiled over on a number of occasions into violent race riots.

David Bowie lived for a period as an outsider in LA, before leaving with some very negative impressions. In the biography *Alias David Bowie*, Peter and Leni Gillman suggest part of the reason for the singer's personality crisis of the mid-1970s was 'the malign influence of Los Angeles itself. With its vast, random sprawl, its network of helter-skelter freeways, its lack of anything that could be called a city centre, its garish newness, its population of attention-seekers, its worship of the entertainment industry and all its attendant fantasies, it was perhaps the least suitable place on earth for a person to go in search of identity and stability. Later on David was to express his feelings about Los Angeles with vitriolic passion. It was, David said, "the most vile piss-pot in the whole world . . . It's a movie that is so corrupt with a script that is so devious and insidious. It's the scariest movie ever written. You feel a total victim there, and you know someone's got the strings on you."'

LA formed part of the inspiration for *Mechanical Animals*, Marilyn Manson's musical comment on the emptiness of fame, as did Bowie himself. 'Moving to Hollywood, I experienced a rebirth,' recalls Marilyn. 'I'd stripped away all my emotions in the past and I started to get them back. Living in this strange city I felt almost like a child or an alien, and the more I got my emotions back, the more I saw that the rest of the world had less and less. I started seeing people as the mechanical animals I talk about on the record.'

On another occasion, he sought to describe the city's homestate. 'California's just too complicated to explain in one conversation. It's best described as – from where I live on the hill, looking down on the city, it's like floating in space. Even the stars seem below you – it can be very depressing. So there'll be a lot on this record about the darkness behind the California smile.' LA now looks set to figure large in the Marilyn Manson film project *Holy Wood*, which sounds intriguingly close to the metaphorical movie that Bowie described.

LOOKING FORWARD WITH ANGER

Kenneth Anger is an intriguing presence on the shadowy fringes of American culture, representing an axis between golden-age Hollywood glamour, rock-god excess, hippie mysticism and the curious philosophies of Aleister Crowley. He first drew the public eye as a child actor in the 1935 version of *A Midsummer Night's Dream*, but was not destined for mainstream Hollywood – as his first directorial project, the 1942 short film *Fireworks* demonstrates. A violent homo-erotic fantasy, it features Anger in the lead role as a homosexual who dreams of being beaten up by a gang of sailors. America wasn't ready for such provocation, but the young director gained a number of admirers in the international avant-garde community, particularly in France, and by the mid-1950s was a respected underground film-maker.

Anger's 'Magick Lantern Cycle' consists of nine films made between 1942 and 1980: some are dominated by threatening homo-erotic themes (like the strange 1963 biker flick *Scorpio Rising*), while others evoke the atmosphere of the lost Hollywood of the 1920s (most notably the 1949 short *Puce Moment*). Most, however, are Crowley-style rituals captured on celluloid, like the 1954 *Inauguration of the Pleasure Dome*.

Anger quotes from Crowley in his celebrated Tinseltown exposé, *Hollywood Babylon*, and the influence of the late English poet and sorcerer can be felt in almost everything this volatile, temperamental artist does. During the 1960s he became a familiar figure in San Francisco, heart of the hippie movement, mingling with its colourful denizens, including hippie-hating Anton LaVey, who recruited Anger as a founder member of the Church of Satan. Anger drew parallels between the hippies' 'Age of Aquarius' and the Aeon of Horus Crowley had predicted. He also interpreted it as the 'Aeon of Lucifer', citing Crowley's Luciferian maxim that 'the key to joy is disobedience'.

The occult glamour his Crowleyan beliefs conferred upon him also attracted the attention of some of the rock world's more daring souls. In the late 1960s he was briefly unofficial magus to the Rolling Stones, inspiring their flirtation with the demonic which produced the song 'Sympathy for the Devil'. He later collaborated with Jimmy Page, guitarist with Led Zeppelin, who shared Anger's fascination with the Great Beast. Neither of Anger's high-profile musical associations ended very amicably, though accounts as to why vary wildly.

The reasons for Anger's split with one of his hippie proteges are better known. He met Bobby Beausoleil, a handsome young hippie drifter, in San Francisco during 1965. The film-maker decided his new acquaintance was perfect for the leading role in his short film *Lucifer Rising*. However, this original version of the film was never completed for, in 1967, his Lucifer stole the footage Anger had shot and headed south towards Los Angeles, where he met ex-jailbird hippie Charlie Manson and joined the strange commune many were calling 'the Family'.

In 1969, Beausoleil stabbed music teacher and small-time drug dealer Gary Hinman to death. Some claim it was his arrest for this crime that inspired the Manson murders, perpetrated as copy-cat crimes to try and prove the real perpetrator of the Hinman slaying was still at large. Others believe that the curse Kenneth Anger very publicly placed on Beausoleil after the hippie fled San Francisco – inscribing a medallion with a toad and Beausoleil's name – assured ill fortune for its target.

Celluloid sorcery - Kenneth Anger's Inauguration of the Pleasure Dome.

Whatever the truth of the matter, it's incontestable that Kenneth Anger remains the only figure thus far to marry the magic of the traditional sorcerer with the power of the rock idol and the glamour of the silver screen. Now that Marilyn Manson intends to do the same, it was inevitable that these two larger-than-life mavericks would eventually meet (in late 1999). While Marilyn continues to cite Anger as an inspirational cinematic influence, it remains to be seen whether these two very powerful egos will ever actually collaborate.

a penitent Wilde had solicited an audience with the Pope.

Debate still rages as to just how sincere Wilde's conversion was – whether the supreme poseur was simply striking another pose. Like Marilyn Manson, however, Oscar Wilde had confessed to an early admiration of *The Bible* on his own typically idiosyncratic terms, observing, 'When I think of all the harm that book has done, I despair of ever writing anything to equal it.' Also like Marilyn, he subversively described the holy scriptures as a storybook: 'Do you know, *The Bible* is a wonderful book. How beautifully artistic the little stories are!' Verging on blasphemy, he didn't revere Christ so much as identify with him as 'the supreme artist'. As Ellis Hanson observes in *Decadence and Catholicism*, Wilde regarded Jesus as 'a great work of art, the ultimate object of aestheticism, a poetic icon whole and in himself, a Christ for Christ's sake'.

Perhaps most shocking to the pious was Wilde's tendency to project his own homosexuality onto his version of Christ. 'The homoeroticism of discipleship was by no means lost on Wilde,' writes Hanson, 'who was evidently delighted by Frank Harris's [the famous pornographer's] interpretation of Judas's betrayal as the act of a jealous lover who thought himself abandoned for "that sentimental beast John."' Like those blasphemous Decadents who regarded Jesus as an object of homosexual desire, Wilde even compared Christ to Lord Alfred Douglas ('Bosie'), the aristocrat with whom he had enjoyed the homosexual affair that led to his arrest and imprisonment. 'Wilde struggled to see the lovely figure of Christ even in the slim-gilt body of Lord Alfred Douglas,' says Hanson. 'On the eve of his sentencing – his own martyrdom – he wrote a love letter to Douglas, claiming that the boy had Christ's own heart.' Wilde converted because he saw a parallel between his own persecution and that of Christ, ignoring the fact that, according to biblical lore, Christ's martyrdom was a noble self-sacrifice, while *The Bible* prescribes death for the 'crime' of homosexuality.

Just as Oscar Wilde saw a reflection of himself in Christ, so Marilyn Manson has compared himself to the decadent Irishman, claiming, 'We were both persecuted for our beliefs.' While on his way to Reading gaol, Wilde was forced to wait on a train platform while crowds jeered and spat at him, later comparing this salvo of spit to the abuse suffered by Christ as he made his way to his execution. Perhaps this is why Marilyn Manson encourages the audience to spit at his shows – an act of self-conscious (or possibly sub-conscious) self-martyrdom.

So where will Marilyn Manson go in this new millennium? Marilyn himself has hinted at a new persona, his previous identities strewn behind him like skins shed by a luridly sinister snake. Gone is the drug-crazed childhood villain of *Portrait of an American Family*; gone the Nietzschean fallen angel of *Antichrist Superstar*; imminent is the demise of the androgynous space-age decadent of *Mechanical Animals*. The release of his first retrospective live album and video draws a line under the first phase of the 'science project' that is Marilyn Manson. 'I reinvent myself before I can get bored of myself,' he observed in a recent interview. 'Anyone who remains static is not only unimaginative but is being safe. The real safe thing for me would be to make another album like *Antichrist Superstar*, look the same way I looked, and say the same things in interviews. But I've grown tired of that. There's lots more to explore.'

In December of 1999, Marilyn announced via his website that Omega had been 'disposed of, as he was a ruse to lure commercial mall-goers into the web of destruction'. His new persona, identified only by the alchemical symbol for mercury, came clad in spartan black, shaved bald, his eyes and lips outlined in ebony – resembling a more glamorous version of Uncle Fester from camp gothic favourite movie *The Addams Family*, or, more poignantly, the lead figure in the 1981 film of Klaus Mann's novel *Mephisto*. (As in the original story of *Faust*, who sold his soul to Mephistopheles, the Devil, for knowledge and pleasure, in *Mephisto* the actor Hendrik Hofgen sells his principles and humanity to the Nazis in 1940s Germany. Hiding behind applause, the most memorable of the series of masks he wears is that of the white-faced Devil.)

In the same Internet broadcast, Marilyn announced the title of his upcoming fourth album as *In the Shadow of the Valley of Death*, identifying it as 'the final piece of a triptych that I began with *Antichrist Superstar*'. In an earlier interview, he explained that 'It's probably the darkest and most violent music we've ever done. We took the melodic rock arrangements on *Mechanical Animals* and combined them with the more nihilistic approach that *Antichrist Superstar* had. The synthesis of the two is beautiful.'

Perhaps more significant than its connection to the two previous albums is the role that *In the Shadow of the Valley of Death* will play as a companion piece, or introduction, to Marilyn Manson's most ambitious project to date. 'It contains songs that will hint at the story that will be told in my film *Holy Wood*,' he recently revealed. 'It's all really a metaphor for my own life, but the story, without giving away too much, takes place in an alternate dystopia of Hollywood where everything is taken to the extreme,' reveals Marilyn. 'It's sort of Andy Warhol's worst nightmare, combined with scientology and communism. If you imagined everything was as far as anyone can take it, the way movie stars are treated. There are a lot of references to the way that I see John F. Kennedy as a modern day Christ and how religion kind of sprouts from that. It's a really strange story, but in the end it's a parable about fame and love and what matters to you the most . . .'

'In a sense it's very Shakespearean. It's a very traditional story but the way I'm going to tell it is with extreme, never-before-seen images, never-before-heard-of concepts. I wanted to have a very traditional story so people don't get lost. The way I show violence in this film will be in a way that no one has ever seen . . . It's going to make people re-evaluate their feelings on violence. It's going to make them really wonder whether they're hating it or glorifying it.'

As ever, the almost megalomaniacal intention is to create a work of art rather than just a product. 'I'm going to show people that I have a really new outlook on religion.

WRAPPED IN PLASTIC

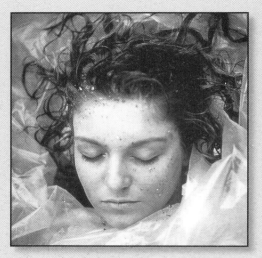

Laura Palmer (Sheryl Lee) 'wrapped in plastic' - the corpse at the core of David Lynch's cult Twin Peaks *TV show.*

Maverick film director David Lynch's work has been a long-time pre-occupation of Marilyn Manson. Lynch has mastered the difficult act of achieving some success in Hollywood while retaining his own unique vision and style, both quintessentially American and disconcertingly alien. After a couple of surreal shorts, Lynch made *Eraserhead* (1977), a celluloid nightmare of frightening absurdity. It attracted the attention of comedy legend Mel Brooks who contracted Lynch to direct *The Elephant Man* (1980), the story of a Victorian freak as beautiful on the inside as he was physically deformed on the outside. Its box-office success and eight Academy Award nominations established Lynch as a director to be reckoned with.

After the science fiction epic *Dune* (1984), a bloated, over-ambitious if underrated mess, Lynch redeemed himself with *Blue Velvet* (1986), his unforgettable gothic-*noir* thriller. *Wild at Heart* (1990) followed, a lurid, sprawling road movie saturated with Lynch's hallucinatory directorial style. As if predicting the style of Marilyn Manson, *Wild At Heart* blended adult themes (graphic sex and violence) with classic images taken from children's entertainment (the 1939 film *The Wizard of Oz* being an obvious influence).

However, most people know David Lynch best through his work on the small screen – specifically the cult hit *Twin Peaks*, a TV series that gave the traditional American murder mystery the distinctive, delirious Lynch treatment. (The Twin Peaks world was later supplemented with a full-length 1992 feature film, *Fire Walk With Me*.) The agonised murmur of the character who finds the body of murdered high school homecoming queen Laura Palmer – 'She's all wrapped in plastic . . .' – is echoed in the Marilyn Manson song of the same name. In 'Wrapped in Plastic', images of temptation and corruption weave through a sinister image which seems to suggest Laura Palmer's relationship with her incestuous, murderous father: 'Daddy tells the daughter while Mommy's sleeping at night / To wash away sin you must take off your skin. / The righteous father wears the yellowest grin.'

Marilyn Manson scored his Hollywood debut in Lynch's next movie, *Lost Highway* (1996), where he plays a sleazily sinister sleazy porn star alongside Twiggy Ramirez and contributed two songs to the soundtrack, 'Apple of Sodom' and his cover of Screamin' Jay Hawkins' 'I Put a Spell on You'. (The soundtrack features a number of Manson influences and associates, including Nine Inch Nails, David Bowie and the Smashing Pumpkins.) A dark, deranged, almost psychotic thriller, *Lost Highway* is vintage Lynch.

The creative affinity between the wholesome misfit film director and the androgynous sleazoid rock star is born out by the brief, epigrammatic introduction to *The Long Hard Road Out of Hell*, in which a cryptic Lynch opines that 'He [Marilyn] was beginning to look and sound a lot like Elvis.'

Lynch's next TV project, a proposed series entitled *Mulholland Drive*, was also set to feature Marilyn Manson, but the ABC network pulled the plug on the pilot film because it was too 'strange and violent'. This current climate of concern over violence in the media was created in no small part by the tabloid witch-hunt that followed the Columbine massacre. However, Manson and Lynch seem destined to collaborate further, and Marilyn has put the director forward as potential helmsman on his *Holy Wood* project.

The other candidate suggested by Marilyn is ex-*Monty Python* team-member Terry Gilliam. During his career as a director, Gilliam has covered many of the themes dear to Marilyn's heart, including surreal children's tales with an acidic edge – *Time Bandits* (1981) – and dystopian futuristic fantasies – *Brazil* (1985). Marilyn has singled out Gilliam's movie *Fear and Loathing in Las Vegas* (1998) for special praise, describing it as 'the very first movie that exactly captured the drug feeling. I was high just from watching!'

SPLATTER AND SYMBOLISM

Russian-Chilean director/actor Alexandro Jodorowsky is one of those rare film-makers who is more fascinatingly bizarre than any of his more extreme celluloid creations. Also a reputed comic-book writer, artist, and, some claim, a visionary – he once reflected, 'Maybe I am a prophet. I really hope one day there will come Confucius, Mohammed, Buddha, and Christ to see me. And we will sit at a table, taking tea and eating some brownies' – his films have split the international critical community into those who regard his work as brilliantly unique, and the greater mass of mainstream opinion which dismisses it as exploitative and incoherent. 'I ask of film what most North Americans ask of psychedelic drugs,' he once explained of the cult films that have certainly found a ready audience among drug-takers.

THE DEFINITIVE CULT SPAGHETTI WESTERN

"If you're great, 'El Topo' is a great picture.
If you're limited, 'El Topo' is limited."
A. Jodorowsky

EL TOPO

A FILM BY ALEXANDRO JODOROWSKY

18

El Topo (1969), which many regard as his masterpiece, has been described by Marilyn Manson as his favourite movie of all time. When it hit the USA in 1971, it became a huge success with counterculture audiences – *The Los Angeles Free Press* called it 'the greatest film ever made', an opinion echoed by John Lennon. This is particularly striking as, while the film is filled with strange, trippy scenes conforming to the hippie aesthetic, it is also bathed in intense violence. Described by some critics as a 'Zen western', it features the lead character's (played by Jodorowsky) bloodthirsty and surreal quest for vengeance across a bleak Mexican landscape.

Jodorowsky's other rare excursions into cinema include *The Holy Mountain* (1973), described as his 'mescaline movie', featuring nine disciples hoping to discover the secret of eternal life. Their guru (played by Jodorowsky) recounts various bizarre and macabre tales which feature such memorable images as giggling children crucifying Christ, and the conquest of Mexico retold with toads playing the Spanish invaders. *Santa Sangre* (1989) is a serial killer movie given the unmistakable Jodorowsky treatment. A phantasmagoria of carnival freaks, gore, brutality and deranged symbolism, it's a strange but powerful cinematic brew.

Jodorowsky's film-making techniques – and indeed his personality – are reputedly just as eccentric as his films. He uses handicapped people, hookers and passers-by as often as regular actors, filming in crime-ridden slums, turning the whole film-making process into something closer to a spiritual quest than an artistic endeavour. In late 1999 he met with Marilyn Manson in Dublin, in order for the two iconoclasts to discuss working together. There are powerful, if far from obvious, connections between the two artists' work (for example, in *El Topo* Jodorowsky implies that America is the modern counterpart of Hell). Jodorowsky is a far from prolific film-maker, but if he does decide to collaborate with Marilyn, the results are bound to be colourfully compelling and extremely strange.

KILLING FOR CHRIST

The powerful image at the centre of Manson's Last Tour on Earth - Christian or anti-Christian?

Marilyn Manson once observed, 'If you want to blame rock music for things, think about what *The Bible* has done. What about Heaven's Gate or Jim Jones or the Ku Klux Klan? What they do in the name of Christ.'

While killers with alleged satanic connections regularly feature in the mass media, murderers motivated by their Christian beliefs do not receive the same scrutiny. Both in lunatic asylums and on death row, for every inmate who thinks they have a hot-line to Hell there are several who believe they have Heaven's divine sanction.

For example, blood-drinking murderer John George Haigh, 'the Acid-Bath Killer', was partially inspired by the blood symbolism of holy communion, but this was suppressed at his trial. And perhaps the most spectacularly appalling example was Albert Fish, who lent his name to Marilyn Manson band-member Ginger Fish. At his arrest in 1934, Fish was connected to many violent sexual attacks on children across the USA. Most vilely, he also ate pieces of a little girl's body and sent a taunting letter to her grieving parents. Fish was assisted in his crimes by his appearance – he looked every inch the kindly grandfather – and had been apprehended and released on more than one occasion because authorities couldn't believe that a 'sweet old man' could be a child molester.

His motive seems to have been the expression of an extreme sadomasochistic sexuality. Fish loved being savagely beaten with a paddle studded with nails, and enjoyed watching the suffering of others almost as much. He approached the electric chair with anticipation, believing it to be 'the supreme thrill', but the first attempt to fry Fish was thwarted when needles inserted in his own scrotum short-circuited the chair.

Behind this perversity was a deep, demented piety. Fish, who carved crosses into himself, would shriek 'I am Christ!' while in reveries of pain. He was obsessed with punishment and purity, believing that his murder of the little girl, Grace Budd, was somehow 'holy' as he claimed that she died a virgin. All the Christian faith's masochistic hatred of pleasure, pathological fear of sex, unhealthy obsession with innocence and desire for martyrdom appear to have been embodied in Albert Fish. It was not a pretty sight.

JFK

JFK as a cultural icon in this hispanic true crime comic about his assassination.

President John F. Kennedy has become one of the most significant figures of twentieth-century America, an icon of political idealism and lost innocence. After fighting a charismatic, TV-led campaign, Kennedy took power in January 1961 as the youngest-ever president in the White House. Incumbent for less than three years, an assassin's bullet ended his life in November 1963, whereupon he entered the public consciousness as a political martyr. The handsome young war hero's efforts to attack corruption at home, and improve relations abroad, had led the darkest forces in American society to destroy him.

But there is also a dark side to JFK himself. Despite his reputation as a conciliatory leader, the world was closer to nuclear war and global annihilation under Kennedy than at any other point before or since. While he publicly fought corruption, he belonged to a political dynasty that manipulated power behind the scenes for decades, and that some allege had Mafia connections. Indeed, some suggest the conspiracy behind Kennedy's shooting was composed not of American reactionaries, or Cuban radicals, but Mafia 'capi' who believed the President was inadequately repaying their assistance. Kennedy's personal life was not beyond scandal either – his affair with Marilyn Manson's namesake, the legendary Monroe, led to rumours that she was murdered by the security services to maintain her silence.

Kennedy is alluded to a number of times in *Mechanical Animals*, and promises to feature in *Holy Wood*. In a recent interview, Marilyn Manson portrayed Kennedy as a Christ-like figure. 'My theory, that I've really been thinking about since I had so much interaction with Christianity after doing *Antichrist Superstar*, is that Christ was the blueprint for celebrity. He was the first celebrity or rock star, if you want to look at it that way, and he became this image of sexuality and suffering. He's literally marketed. A crucifix is no different than a concert shirt in some ways. I think for America, in my lifetime, John F. Kennedy kind of took the place of that in some ways. He became lifted up as this icon and this Christ figure. I started to – in my weird, drugged version of Hollywood – dream up a world where these dead stars are really saints. Jackie Onassis is kind of like Mary Immaculate. That's what I was thinking when I was writing the album, and I hinted that in a lot of songs, like "Posthuman".'

I have a true belief in Christ in a different sense than Christianity has portrayed. I have a different interpretation of Jehovah, the Old Testament God, than people have portrayed. And a different interpretation of Satan . . . I've taken a lot of my inspiration from Kenneth Anger, Philip K. Dick, J. G. Ballard: people who took very powerful symbolic ideas and took the time to really see what makes the world go round.'

Perhaps the most significant of these figures, in terms of inspiration for *Holy Wood*, will be Anger: 'I want to make something that really raises the standard in the way that someone like Kenneth Anger did in his time,' insists Marilyn. A highly respected underground film-maker, and one of the most important disciples of Aleister Crowley alive today, Anger is acclaimed among art-film aficionados for his Magick Lantern Cycle – a series of short films combining his passion for celluloid and sorcery, capturing Crowleyan ritual on screen. (While these distinctive, visually powerful films attracted underground attention, Anger came to popular prominence with his scandalous 1975 exposé of golden-age film-star excess *Hollywood Babylon*, described as 'a book as legendary as its subject'.)

Crowley figures ever more prominently in Marilyn Manson's world-view, perhaps moreso these days than Anton LaVey, or his Church of Satan. He is more apt to compare his position to that of the Great Beast than to either Wilde or Christ, observing of his scapegoating for the Columbine High massacre: 'It's like Aleister Crowley who, in his time, was destroyed by the press. They called him a Satan worshipper when he was one of the greatest philosophers and magicians of his time.' Crowley attempted to become, in the words of John Lennon, 'bigger than Jesus'; he created a new religion that was supposed to wipe the last remnants of Christianity from the planet with his dogma of 'do as thou wilt'. Could it be that the new millennium will see the dawning of his Aeon of Horus, as evangelised with increasing frequency by the charismatic Marilyn Manson?

His July 1999 message to the Spooky Kids at least suggests the possibility. 'You are a slave,' begins the communication. 'Even Christ wouldn't kill himself for this pitiful America that hides under "Christian values" . . . It's time for their world to be destroyed. It is time for a new age, the Age of Horus. It is time for a new standard, a new canvas, and a new artist. We must forget this wasted generation and amputate it before the mind rots away with it . . .' Signed, 'The third and final beast Marilyn Manson.'

Crowley was known as the Great Beast, but the identify of the 'second beast' remains obscure. Was it Kenneth Anger? Anton LaVey? Whatever, Marilyn Manson makes an intriguing candidate for the inheritor of Crowley's anti-Christian mantle, anticipated by few in the occult community. Deliberately isolating himself from humanity, turning his website into a refuge – his own Abbey of Thelema in cyberspace – Manson's Mercury blurs the lines between cyberpunk sorcerer and multi-media messiah.

His interview pronouncements reveal an increasingly Crowleyan philosophy, influencing his predictions for the future. 'Now that everyone has the ability to be a star it's gonna get to the stage in the next few years where the really talented people and the really strong-willed people will come to the forefront and really lead the world into something stronger,' he proclaims. 'All of the mediocre people who are riding on luck will be cast aside. I think I'm a rival to religion and a rival to politics and people prefer you to feel strongest about those things. Kids feel stronger about something else so it becomes dangerous to everyone.'

More ominous for his opponents, and most intriguing for his fans, Marilyn Manson has declared, 'In some ways Christianity should thank me and in some ways they should hate me, because I'm really going to pull the curtain down on them. And not in the way they expect me to.'